Mirror Gazing:

Predict the future

Look into the past

Unlock your creativity

Mirror Gazing:

Predict the future
Look into the past
Unlock your creativity

Irene McGarvie

Ancient Wisdom Publishing
a division of Nixon-Carre Ltd., Toronto, ON

Copyright © 2010 by Irene McGarvie

All rights reserved. No part of this book may be reproduced or transmitted in any form or by any means, electronic or mechanical, including photocopying and recording, or by any information storage or retrieval system without written permission from the author, except for brief passages quoted in a review.

Library and Archives Canada Cataloguing in Publication

McGarvie, Irene, 1957-
　　Mirror gazing : predict the future, look into the past, unlock your creativity / Irene McGarvie.

Includes index.
ISBN 978-1-926826-01-1

　　1. Crystal gazing. 2. Divination. I. Title.

BF1335.M33 2010　　　　133.3'22　　　　C2010-903174-1

Published by: Ancient Wisdom Publishing
(A division of Nixon-Carre Ltd.)
P.O. Box 92533 Carlton RPO
Toronto, Ontario, M5A 4N9

www.learnancientwisdom.com
www.nixon-carre.com

Distributed by Ingram 1-800-937-8000
www.ingrambook.com

Cover image: www.istockphoto.com

Disclaimer:
This publication is sold with the understanding that the publishers are not engaged in rendering legal, medical or other professional advice. The information contained herein represents the experiences and opinions of the author, but the author or the publisher are not responsible for the results of any action taken on the basis of information in this work, nor for any errors or omissions.

Printed and bound in the USA

Contents

Chapter 1 - What is mirror gazing? 1
How does it work? • Can we control the information we receive? • Can anyone do it? • Everyone has had a psychic experience • Scrying tools or "speculum" • The "Astral" plane • A link to another level of reality • Are the visions "real" or just hallucinations?

Chapter 2 - Scrying throughout history 11
Every culture has practiced some form of scrying • Ancient Greece • Hawaiian Islands • Ancient Persia • Kenneth MacKenzie • Nostradamus • Dr. John Dee • Edward Kelly • The Enochian or Angelic language • Count Cagliostro • The Mormon "seer stones" • Abraham Lincoln • Harry Potter

Chapter 3 - What to expect 23
• Seeing with your mind • Cloud patterns • Vague, then becoming more vivid • Relaxed expectation • Symbolism • Touch, taste, smell • Sounds • Controlling the session • Setting your intention • Meeting and talking with deceased loved ones • Meet spirit guides and angels • Spirit Mentors • Lost objects or missing persons • Improve your creativity • Explore past lives • Understand yourself better • Remote viewing • See the past, present, and future • Develop your psychic abilities • The Legend of Narcissus

Chapter 4 - Where do the visions come from? . . . 41

Is mirror gazing dangerous? • Where do the visions come from? • Contradictions in Christianity & Judaism • The subconscious or unconscious mind • Carl Jung and the collective unconscious • The super-conscious mind • Archetypes • Time travel • Layers of reality • The "middle realm" • Do we need protection? • Trickster spirits • Whatever you send out you will get back • Do you have to "believe" in order for it to work?

Chapter 5 - Preparing your tools 61

• Make your own inexpensive scrying mirror • Consecrating your mirror • Setting up your scrying location • Keep your tools covered when not in use • Scrying in water • Mesmerism and magnetic energy • Crystal balls • Choosing a crystal ball • Clear or colored crystal? • Building a modern psychomanteum • Setting up your mirror

Chapter 6 - The importance of ritual 79

• A simple ritual • A clean room • Clean clothes • A clean body • Salt • Water • Prayer • Incense • Candles • Soft music • Ending the ritual and "closing" yourself off • More elaborate rituals • Fasting • Alcohol • Sexual energy • The "magic" is inside you

Chapter 7 - How to do it 89

Collect your tools • Set up your space • Perform your ritual • Silence • Meditation music • Positioning your mirror • A bowl of water • Incense • Light your candles

• Relaxed expectation • The self hypnotic state • How often should you scry • Give the universe some advance notice • Consider what you eat • Scrying with a partner • Keep a scrying journal

Chapter 8 - Exercises to improve your ability ... 101
• Do you have to be gifted? • Everyone gets "hunches" • A psychic aristocracy • Male vs. female • What if you can't visualize? • Training the mind • Monkey mind • Exercises • Simple objects • Morphing shapes • Rose bud • Morphing numbers • Spirit body exercise • Your secret place • Exploring your private world • Memories of past events • Some people are naturals

Appendix A - *"How To Read the Crystal"* 119
by Sepharial
• Who was Sepharial? • The Crystal • Warning • Preliminaries • The Vision • Difficulties • Symbols • Some Experiences • Directions for using the spheres

Appendix B - *"Crystal Gazing and Clairvoyance"* . . 145
by John Melville
• Hints on the use of the crystal • Appearances in the crystal

Appendix C - *"Hygienic Clairvoyance"* 159
by Jacob Dixon
• Clairvoyance: Its Theory and Practice • Magnetic Clairvoyance • Inducing Clairvoyance • What proportion of persons can become clairvoyant

"The supernatural is the natural not yet understood."

Elbert Hubbard

What is mirror gazing?

Mirror gazing is a form of scrying. Scrying is simply a method of divination where you use a tool to see things psychically. You can scry with many different tools, but mirror gazing refers specifically to looking into a darkened mirror to see visions.

Mirror gazing is a technique that can be used by anyone to help develop their psychic or mediumistic abilities. But it can do so much more than that, mirror gazing can enable you to:

- See the past, present, and future
- Ease grief through contact with deceased loved ones
- Meet your spirit guides and angels
- Gain knowledge from the spirit realm through visions
- Experience astral projection, have an out-of-body experience
- Explore past lives or future possibilities
- Find solutions to business or personal problems
- Look for hidden objects, or missing persons
- Improve your creativity
- Understand yourself better

Mirror gazing/scrying is a technique that has been used by prophets, mystics, and inventors throughout the centuries. It has been described as a technique for purposefully inducing waking hallucinations. But most people who have experienced it are very reluctant to describe it as just a self-induced hallucination. The experience can range from simply watching a slide show of images taking place in the mirror in front of you, to finding yourself transported to another time and place. It can feel like you are imagining it, or it can feel as real as your everyday life. I have sometimes heard it described as "more real than real life."

For centuries Christian churches have condemned mirror gazing as satanic or evil, and yet many Biblical figures used a form of it to receive Divine guidance. So which is it, a useful skill or a demonic tool? Obviously, I think that it is a useful skill that anyone can learn.

I became fascinated with the idea of scrying when I was a young girl as a result of stories I had heard from my mother and grandmother of people who could see visions in polished stones. My grandmother gave me a ptarmigan claw kilt pin inlaid with some sort of semi-precious stone when I was about 10 years old and told me that if I practiced maybe I would be able to use it to see visions. My father was very uncomfortable with this and when my grandmother went home to Scotland he demanded that the kilt pin be put away until I was older, and I don't know what became of it.

I was terribly disappointed thinking that my ability to scry was dependent on some special stone or expensive crystal ball, and these sorts of things were not readily available in the small town where I grew up. It wasn't until I grew up and found out that an inexpensive picture frame would work just as well that the wonderful world of mirror gazing opened up to me.

How does it work?

Unlike what I thought as a child, there is no magic in mirror gazing, it is basically a form of self hypnosis. Focusing on a mirror, a crystal ball, or any other shiny surface helps you to concentrate your attention and enables you to go into an altered state. While in this state you are able to access information that is not normally available to your conscious mind.

Most of the time we are too busy with our daily activities to notice or tap into any extra sensory information. I think that for most of us, the spirits of our deceased loved ones could be doing a tap dance in front of us and we wouldn't notice. Our unconscious mind could be attempting to show us the simple solution to a problem but because we are so tied up in our day to day problems we are unable to access the answers and so we just continue to struggle along.

It is true that occasionally, usually at times of extreme need, the unconscious mind can break through into our conscious awareness to give us important information, but most of the time we just fumble along in the darkness. But it doesn't have to be this way.

Can we control the information we receive?

To some extent we can influence what we are hoping to achieve during our mirror gazing session by consciously setting our purpose. Setting your purpose is not complicated.

It can be as simple as just stating out loud what you are hoping to achieve. The spoken word is a very powerful tool. Our thoughts are often jumbled, but when you speak the thought out loud you are better able to focus on what it is you really want.

Putting your intention down in writing also helps you to focus. Narrowing your focus in this way is like light streaming through a magnifying glass. It condenses your focus and makes it much more powerful.

Sometimes when we sit down to mirror gaze, even though we have clearly set out our intention, the vision we get is not what we were expecting. While we may not get what we expect we always get what we need. It often happens that you sit down to mirror gaze hoping to speak to a particular loved one and are startled instead to find yourself conversing with someone else. Maybe the person you were hoping to see was not available, or more likely, your higher self (or your higher power?) knew that there were more pressing issues that needed to be resolved.

Can anyone do it?

Mirror gazing is a form of self hypnosis and anyone who can induce within themselves the suggestible state of self hypnosis can learn to do it. Many authors claim that only a certain percentage of the population can be hypnotized, but I disagree. We all daydream, and we all go into light trance states regularly, and this is all you need to be able to get messages from your unconscious through the mirror. Unless you have a brain injury that inhibits your ability to remember or visualize things you will be able to mirror gaze.

You might not become as gifted as Nostradamus, but anyone with the desire can learn to scry to some degree.

Everyone has had a psychic experience

Everyone has had a psychic experience of some kind. Everyone has experienced déjà vu, the sense that you have experienced something before. Who hasn't had the experience of hearing someone say their name when no one else was around? Who hasn't experienced seeing something out of the corner of your eye but when you turn to look there was nothing there.

Tapping into the unseen realm is something that we all do regularly. But most people are reluctant to talk about their psychic experiences out of fear of what people will think, but everyone has had them.

For example, a friend of mine, a very skeptical man, described a startling experience he had while attending the funeral of a friend.

Sitting in the church during the funeral service he was startled to see his deceased friend standing at the back of the church watching the events. Confused, my friend describes how he quietly got up from his pew and walked back to the lobby of the church where he had a conversation with the deceased man! They had a regular, somewhat casual conversation. They discussed the number of people who had turned out for the funeral, talked about golf, just mundane things like that, nothing particularly profound, and then as the service was ending my friend headed back to his seat and the deceased man disappeared. Of course, my friend wishes now that he had thought to ask the deceased man about more important matters, like exactly what happens when you die, but regardless, he found the experience life changing because now he is sure, beyond a shadow of a doubt, that even though the body was in the coffin, the personality of the person remained.

Needless to say, my friend has been extremely reluctant to tell anyone, especially anyone at work, about his experience because it sounds so far fetched.

I can't begin to list the number of people who have told me that they have been visited by a deceased loved one. Even the most sensible, practical people that you can imagine have had these experiences.

But these psychic experiences are not limited to contact with the deceased. One woman described to me how she was looking for a job and she just suddenly "saw" herself working at a particular bakery. She got the sudden impulse to go over to the bakery and talk to the owner and just as she arrived the bakery owner was placing a help wanted sign in the window. She got the job and a few years later ended up buying the bakery. Was it a coincidence that she got the impulse to go to that bakery right when the previous owner was looking to hire additional staff? I don't think so.

These experiences that I have just described happened spontaneously, but wouldn't it be great if you could control when these sorts of events take place. Well, to some extent, mirror gazing allows you to deliberately experience these sorts of psychic events.

Scrying tools or "speculum"

A tool used for scrying is called a speculum. For our purposes in this book the tool we are using is the black mirror, but there are lots of other tools that can be used instead.

Candle - it is possible to go into an altered state and see visions in the flame or in the smoke of a candle. A campfire also works very well for this. Some people can even get visions by looking into the smoke emanating from a burning piece of incense.

Crystal ball - this is what most people think of when they think of scrying, the image of an old gypsy woman getting visions by leaning over a clear crystal ball. The crystal ball does not have to be large. I know of people who can get visions in a small crystal pendant hanging around their neck.

Water bowl - scrying in a bowl of water has been a very popular method of receiving visions throughout history. Nostradamus, one of history's most famous scryers, used a bowl of water.

A sword blade or any other shiny surface - there have been numerous accounts throughout history of warriors predicting the outcome of a battle based on visions they saw in their sword blade. A polished finger nail or a shiny ring works well for some people.

A polished stone - as I mentioned earlier, many people scry using a polished stone. It doesn't have to be transparent like a crystal, just as long as it is smooth and shiny. Find a stone that you are particularly drawn to and polish it up. It might prove to be exactly the right tool for you.

So as you can see, mirror gazing or scrying does not require special expensive equipment. The magic is in you, not in the tool.

The "astral" plane

Many people believe that the visions we perceive during mirror gazing take place on the astral plane. The astral plane can be described as another dimension of reality that exists at the same time and place as our conscious reality.

Some people claim that there are 7 levels or dimensions, while others claim that there are 21 levels or 33 levels. Who knows for sure? I am not convinced one way or the other, but it doesn't really matter. The only thing I know with complete certainty is that we live on the physical plane and there are other planes of existence where events are taking place at the same time. Usually we are only consciously aware of the events taking place on the level that we are living on, but it appears that other levels exist at the same time.

So this astral plane where the visions take place, does it exist "just" in our mind? Well sort of, but just because it is taking place in our mind does not mean that it is not real or that it is not really happening. The astral world could be described as being like a layer of consciousness that lies over top of our normal consciousness, like layers of transparent images placed one on top of another.

Back in high school science class I remember we had a teaching aid that was a chart of the human body. It was like a book made of transparent pages. When you peeled back the first page which showed the exterior of the body you saw the muscles under the skin. When you peeled back the page with the muscles on it you saw the circulatory system. When you peeled back that page you saw the internal organs. When you peeled back the next page you saw the skeleton. I think that the various planes of existance are kind of like that book. Generally we only see the page we are on at the moment.

But when we see images in the mirror it is like we are seeing two or more levels of reality at the same time like an image from a movie projector being projected on top of a painting. The two images would appear to be one image, but actually they are separate images being viewed as one.

When we see and interact with those in the spirit realm they appear to be with us in the physical realm, but what we are seeing is taking place on some other level. Sometimes the image is "ghostly" or see-through, while other times it seems very solid.

Scrying creates a link to another level of reality

In effect, what mirror gazing does is allow us to open up a doorway or link to another world, or another dimension of reality. Sometimes this doorway opens up spontaneously like we saw in the earlier examples, but what mirror gazing does is enable us to deliberately open the door to what some people refer to as the "middle realm."

This middle realm could be thought of as a place half way between our physical existence and the spirit world.

Are the visions "real" or just hallucinations?

It is true that in a scrying session we see only with the mind. But just because something is taking place in your mind does not mean that it is not "real." It has often been said that there is nothing supernatural, only huge gaps in our understanding of what is natural.

Let's face it, what do we really "know?" In the past everyone "knew" that the world was flat and that the sun revolved around the earth. How ridiculous will our present day "knowledge" appear to the people of the future.

Scrying throughout history

Every culture has practiced some form of scrying

Throughout history every culture has used some form of scrying tool to access information that is outside of their conscious awareness. For example, the Maoris of New Zealand used a drop of their own blood while the ancient Celts used smooth stones.

Ancient Greece

Pausanius, a second century Greek writer described how sick people would go to see the oracle of the well at the Temple of Ceres at Patras to determine the outcome of their illness.

After praying to the goddess at the temple and giving an offering of incense the sick person would lower a mirror (probably black obsidian stone), suspended by twine, down into the well until it just touched the water. By looking down into the darkness at their reflection in the mirror they knew the outcome of their illness by the image that they saw. If the image appeared strong and healthy they knew that they would recover, but if the image looked ghostly or ill they knew they would die.

Hawaiian Islands

Prior to the introduction of Christianity to the residents of the Hawaiian Islands and other Polynesian Islands by missionaries in the 19th century, if a theft had taken place the local Kahuna or Shaman would dig a hole in the floor of the hut that had been robbed, fill the hole with water, and gaze into the water until he could see the image of the thief. The shaman would then be able to name the guilty person and a suitable punishment could be imposed.

Ancient Persia

In ancient Persia it was believed that practitioners of the mystery sciences could look into a golden cup called the Cup of Jamshid to access information from beyond the physical world.

It was these ancient Persians who came up with the premise that there are seven layers of the universe.

Even the Bible makes reference to using a cup for divination. Genesis 44:5 refers to the cup that the Biblical figure Joseph used to get messages from God.

Famous/Infamous scryers throughout history

Kenneth MacKenzie

Kenneth MacKenzie was a scryer in 15th century Scotland who used a polished stone to get visions. He claimed that his scrying stone was given to him by angels who placed it on his chest when he was sleeping.

Apparently he was particularly adept at remote viewing where he would gaze at his polished stone to see events that were taking place at a distance.

In that period of Scottish history there were many small kingdoms. The story goes that a local queen was worried about her husband's safety while he was away on an extended trip to France and so she asked MacKenzie to look into his stone and see if he could see anything. Not only was the traveling king in good health, but MacKenzie saw him romantically involved with another woman. His mistake was in telling the queen who became so angry that she ordered MacKenzie killed by having him thrown into a cauldron of boiling oil.

Nostradamus

Michel de Nostredame, better known to us as Nostradamus, was a French apothecary (pharmacist) and scryer who made more than a thousand prophecies regarding major world events based on visions that he saw in his scrying bowl.

Nostradamus was born sometime in December of 1503

in Saint-Rémy-de-Provence in the south of France. In 1519 he studied at the University of Avignon for one year until it was forced to close due to an outbreak of the plague. He spent the next few years traveling about the country researching herbal remedies and working as an apothecary. He wanted to study to become a medical doctor but was refused because being an apothecary was deemed to be a manual labor position not worthy of a medical doctor.

The death of his first wife and two children from the plague was probably the catalyst for his goal of developing a treatment for the plague. He ultimately became famous and wealthy through the development of his "rose pill" a herbal remedy that seemed to be effective in preventing the plague. He later remarried a wealthy widow and had six more children.

Freed from financial concerns due to the success of his herbal remedy, and his new wife's money, his interests moved from herbalism to the occult sciences. It was on a trip to Italy sometime around 1550 that he learned how to scry using a large bowl of water. It became his practice to retire to his study and gaze into the bowl of water every night at midnight. Around this time he began publishing almanacs which included his prophesies.

His prophecies were laid out as "quatrains," which are four line rhyming verses, and were primarily written in French. The meanings were obscured by word games and the inclusion of words in other languages. Some researchers claim that he deliberately obscured the meanings because he felt vulnerable to religious attacks, but other researchers suggest that this was unlikely since making predictions was not an offence in the eyes of the Catholic Church at that time.

Although his predictions are rather vague, undated, and difficult to interpret until after the fact, many people believe that Nostradamus' quatrains predicted major world events up to the present day including the French Revolution, the rise and fall of both Napoleon Bonaparte and Adolf Hitler, World Wars I and II, the development of the atomic bomb and destruction of Hiroshima and Nagasaki, the assassination of John F. Kennedy, the Apollo moon landings, and the death of Diana Princess of Wales.

He even prophesied his own death on July 2, 1566. The previous evening he had told his secretary "you will not find me alive at sunrise" and the following morning he was found dead on the floor of his bedroom. Of course that might not have been such a miraculous prediction given that he had been suffering terrible pain from gout which was making it very difficult for him to move around, and as he was an accomplished herbalist it is possible that he had taken something to hasten his passing.

Dr. John Dee

Dr. John Dee (1527 - 1608) was a consultant to Queen Elizabeth I who reigned from 1558-1603. It is generally recognized that she had a strong character and was politically astute, and surrounded herself with competent advisors. The Elizabethan period has been called the Golden Age of England because it was during her reign that England established its naval superiority during the battles against Spain.

Some people claim that it was not naval superiority, rather it was magic in the form of a hex or a curse that was placed on the Spanish Armada by Dr. John Dee that caused the series of misfortunes that sent the Spanish Armada limping back to Spain in defeat. Others claim that through scrying Dee was able to "see" the path of the Spanish ships, predict their military strategy, and outmanoeuvre them.

In using his scrying skills to spy on the Spanish on behalf of the Queen, John Dee was the original James Bond 007. The signature that he apparently used on his confidential correspondence with the Queen was a drawing of a pair of eyeglasses.

He has been called the "last royal magician" because after this time the official belief in "magic" declined and the belief in science took its place.

Dee maintained that he got his information from angels through scrying using a crystal ball that the angels gave him. Other times he used an obsidian mirror which is still on display in the British Museum.

Edward Kelly

Depending on who is telling it, Edward Kelly (1555-1597) was either a con artist or a gifted scryer. Born Edward Talbott, he claimed to have studied at Oxford, but regardless of whether he actually attended university or not, he was an educated man, and knew some Latin and Greek, and according to several accounts he was a gifted forger. Throughout his life he was fascinated with the study of alchemy, the pseudo-science devoted to the turning of base metals into gold.

Kelly contacted John Dee in 1582 offering to assist

him in his metaphysical studies. Dee had been attempting to contact angels through scrying, but was having limited success. Impressed with Kelly's demonstration of his ability, Dee began utilizing Kelly's services as a scryer. From 1582 to 1589 Dee and Kelly worked closely together contacting the spirit world.

Dr. John Dee kept detailed scrying journals recording each session in which he participated with Edward Kelly. Kelly would peer into the crystal ball and Dee would write down everything that Kelly described. Dr. Dee's diaries were published in 1659 under the title *"A True and Faithful Relation of What Passed for Many Years Between Dr. John Dee and Some Spirits."*

The Enochian or Angelic language

Kelly claimed that the angels spoke to him in a special angelic or Enochian language which he was able to understand when he looked into his crystal ball. Kelly claimed that the angels told him that this Enochian language was actually the original form of Hebrew and was the language with which God spoke with Adam.

Some people believe that Kelly simply made up the language as part of an elaborate scam, while others claim that the language was too linguistically elaborate to have been developed by Kelly. Regardless, Dee seems to have sincerely believed that Kelly was actually conversing with angels in an angelic language and not simply making it up.

Dee and Kelly part ways

A falling out between Dee and Kelly occurred in 1587 when Kelly developed an interest in Dee's beautiful young wife and claimed that the angels told him to tell Dee to share her with him. After this experience Dee decided that he would no longer be dependent on another person to do his scrying for him and developed the skill himself.

By 1590, Kelly was living the high life in Europe. He had convinced a number of wealthy and influential people that he was able to produce gold and had been living off their patronage. But eventually they became impatient with his failure to produce and he was imprisoned. Kelly died in 1597. Legend has it that he fell while attempting to escape and died from his injuries.

Count Cagliostro

Giuseppe Balsamo was the real name of Count Alessandro di Cagliostro (1743 - 1795), an Italian con artist and ladies man. Cagliostro claimed to have been of noble birth, but orphaned as a child on the island of Malta. He claimed to have traveled to Egypt where he studied alchemy, the Kabala and magic.

In contrast to the persona he had created, he was actually born to a poor family in Palermo, Sicily and studied chemistry and spiritual rites as a novice in the Catholic Church. He travelled in illustrious circles mingling with European aristocracy, entertaining them and manipulating them with his knowledge of the occult. He was a skilled pharmacist and was even physician to Benjamin Franklin during Franklin's time in Paris.

There are numerous frauds and intrigues associated with Cagliostro, including the famous affair of the diamond necklace which was a scam that involved a forged letter from Marie Antoinette. He was acquitted of these charges due to lack of evidence.

The aspect of Cagliostro's life that interests us is his use of scrying. He was very flamboyant, and performed elaborate scrying rituals in the drawing rooms of his wealthy patrons. It has also been suggested that privately he sometimes used children as seers to get information that he could use to his advantage.

He was apparently adept at what we know of today as remote viewing. Witnesses claimed that he could accurately describe events taking place in other rooms or even across town, and was able to produce hazy ghost like images in the air to illustrate what he was seeing in the crystal or in the mirror. However, this could perhaps be attributed to his ability to hypnotize his audience into believing that they had seen something that did not actually happen.

After spending years living a life of luxury and avoiding conviction for his numerous schemes Cagliostro made the mistake of visiting Rome, where he was turned over to the Inquisition. Some writers claim that it was his wife who betrayed him to the Inquisition as revenge for his numerous romantic liaisons. In 1789 he was arrested and sentenced to death on charges of heresy and of being a Freemason. The Pope ultimately commuted his sentence to life imprisonment. After at least one escape attempt he died in prison at the Fortress of San Leo in 1795.

Was he really an accomplished scryer? Since everyone

is capable of scrying I think it is likely that he was able to see the images he claimed. Did he always use his skill wisely? Probably not. But just because a skill like scrying can be used unwisely or as a means of attempting to defraud, does not mean that it is not a useful skill. Learning how to do it yourself ensures that you are not taken in by con artists claiming to be getting guidance from God or the spirit world.

Joseph Smith Jr. and the Mormon "seer stones"

In the early 1820's Joseph Smith Jr. claimed to have found several "seer stones" that he used for treasure hunting. He would place these stones in his hat and peer into the hat to view the images that would appear on the stones.

Smith founded the Church of Jesus Christ of Latter Day Saints (the Mormons) in the late 1820's based on information he claimed to have received from these stones which he called the Urim and Thummim after the Old Testament stones used by the priests for determining the will of God. Smith claimed to have dictated the text of the Book of Mormon by reading it off the stones in his hat.

Seeing the future on Halloween

In the 19th and early 20th centuries in Europe and in North America there was a popular belief that young women could view the face of their future husband if they gazed into a mirror in a darkened room on Halloween (the one night of the year when it was thought that the veil between the world of spirit and the physical world was particularly thin). However, if they saw a skull which represented death it meant that they would die before they married.

Unintentional mirror gazing

Abraham Lincoln

Abraham Lincoln is reported to have experienced some unintentional mirror gazing. It took place on election night in 1860. On the eve of his re-election, tired after the campaign, he was lounging on a couch in a drawing room of the White House when he saw a double reflection of himself in a nearby mirror. He told his wife Mary, among others, about what he had witnessed and said that he thought it meant that he would be re-elected but would die before the end of his second term. This premonition proved to be accurate.

J.K. Rowling and the Harry Potter phenomena

I remember watching an interview with author J.K. Rowling where she discussed how she came up with the idea for the Harry Potter books. She described sitting on a train heading toward Edinburgh staring blankly out the rain soaked train window as the train rumbled along. She said that she was thinking about a children's book that she wanted to write when suddenly the entire story about the boy wizard played out in her mind from the beginning of the first book right to the end of the entire series.

While Rowling did not claim to be mirror gazing, to those of us who understand how the phenomena works it is obvious what happened. First, she was in a relaxed state. Sitting for a long period of time on the train as it rhythmically clacked along the tracks helped to put her into a self-hypnotic state. The gloomy gray day and the rain soaked windows resulted in a lack of visual sensory input for her brain. She was mulling over plot ideas in her mind and suddenly everything came together.

I am not trying to denigrate her achievement in writing those books. I love the Harry Potter series and I truly admire the skillful way she put it all together, so I am not suggesting that it was just handed to her. She still had to take what she "saw" and write it out. She had been writing and studying literature, history, and mythology for many years when this happened. It is an example of an idea that found its way into a prepared mind.

I love this story about J.K. Rowling's experience because it is an excellent example of how we can use mirror gazing to stimulate creativity and solve problems.

What to expect

Seeing with your mind

If you are sitting in a darkened room and you begin to see images that appear on the darkened surface of an inexpensive picture frame/mirror it is obvious that these images are not a reflection of things that are taking place in the room. Also, since we know that there is no such thing as a magical mirror, there must be a natural explanation for what is happening.

In mirror gazing you see with your mind rather than with your eyes. Normally when you look into a mirror your eyes record the image that is reflected in the mirror and the information (light patterns) are relayed to your brain where they are deciphered and you make sense of what you are seeing. But in mirror gazing it sort of works opposite to this. Rather than interpreting reflected light, your mind creates the image and convinces you that you are viewing it on the darkened surface of the mirror. I realize that this is an oversimplification of how the whole complex process of vision works, but I think this explanation works for our purposes.

Cloud patterns

Mirror gazing visions virtually always start the same way. You are sitting there quietly waiting to see what happens and suddenly you begin to notice the surface of the mirror becoming cloudy. As you become aware of this cloudiness it becomes more vivid.

Vague, then becoming more vivid

Through my own experiences and listening to my students' accounts of their experiences, I have come to the conclusion that it is important to acknowledge the beginning of the cloudiness. When you acknowledge it you will find it becomes more vivid, and when you acknowledge the progression it then morphs into recognizable images, and then the real excitement begins.

I have heard lots of students say *"I didn't see anything, just some cloudiness."*

What I think is happening in their head is that they are thinking, *"I don't see anything, just cloudiness."* By thinking *"I don't see anything,"* they are stopping anything from happening

If instead they thought, *"Oh, the mirror is getting cloudy, now I can see cloud formations,"* then the clouds would more likely turn into an image that they can recognize.

Acknowledging what you are seeing, regardless of how vague it is initially, seems to make the images expand and grow. I have witnessed this many times in mediumship as well as in mirror gazing. By acknowledging that you are seeing some small image causes the image to grow and become more vivid. It is as though the act of acknowledging it serves to fine tune the image, like tuning a radio receiver.

Relaxed expectation

What you expect will affect what you perceive so go into the experience with a sense of relaxed expectation. In other words, know that you will experience something, but don't try to force it or attempt to control what happens or you might end up blocking the experience if you don't immediately experience exactly what you were hoping for.

What will you see?

Sometimes we experience images like a series of still photos, like you are looking through a photo album. These still images can morph into other images. Other times it is more like a movie playing out on a screen in front of you.

But it can also happen that we become part of the action. We can feel like we have been sucked into the mirror and are actually experiencing events in another time and place. Most people wish for this experience since it is particularly useful for remote viewing or time travel, while other people are terrified of experiencing it. But really, there is nothing to be frightened of since you can stop the experience at any time by simply saying no and you will suddenly find yourself back in your seat in the scrying room.

Sometimes the people in the mirror seem to step out of the mirror and come into the room with us. This is wonderful when it happens, but it doesn't happen as often as most of us would like. I'm not sure why it doesn't happen more often but I suspect it requires more energy on the part of the spirit person to do this. A variation of this is where someone comes into the room with you but you don't actually see them, you just sense their presence. This is hard to describe, even though you don't see them you "know" for sure they are there.

Symbolism

We have all heard the expression that "a picture is worth a thousand words." This is often the case with mirror gazing. Sometimes the images we see when mirror gazing are symbolic. It is a form of shorthand. Our mind uses symbols to convey complex information in a way that is meaningful to us. You are unlikely to see images that make absolutely no sense to you.

A particular symbol can mean something very different to different people. For example, to me dogs represent unconditional love and loyalty. The dogs who have shared my life have been my closest friends and companions through some difficult times, but someone who has had bad experiences with dogs will have a different impression when they see a dog. A person who was mauled by a dog as a child will probably feel fear rather than a sense of love, companionship and protection.

A picture of a dog can be symbolic if it just some generic dog (for example, a German Shepherd could represent protection or intelligence, or even danger) or it could be a contact from a deceased pet if the picture is of your particular German Shepherd.

A student in one of my classes was disappointed with her first mirror gazing experience when all that she saw was a peace symbol. But when I asked her what that symbol means to her she immediately understood that it represented the summer of 1969 and all the events that took place for her that summer. In an instant, through seeing that one image, she remembered and understood months of experiences.

Touch, taste or smell

Sometimes you can actually have the sense of touching something, or you can feel someone around you. Other times you might experience a taste in your mouth or have the sensation of smelling something. I find that I get a lot of information given to me through the sense of smell. I often find that I can know what a spirit did for a living, or what was significant to them based on what I smell. For example one man showed me that he was a cook by giving me a strong smell of bacon and eggs cooking.

Sounds

I realize that it seems odd that looking into a mirror can result in "hearing" sounds or voices but it definitely can. If there is no external sound in the room obviously you are not "hearing" it with your ears, but it feels like you are. We all know what our own internal dialogue sounds like, in other words, what it sounds like when you are talking to yourself.

In mirror gazing sometimes it can sound like our own internal dialog, but other times it can be very different. You can hear a person's voice, or the sound of the wind, or street noises, not like you are remembering how these things sound, but actually hearing them as though they were present in the room at the moment.

Is hearing voices like this something that you should be worried about? Does it mean that you are becoming schizophrenic? No, not at all. The thing to remember is that you control whether or not you hear these things, and you decide what you want to do with the information you receive. You don't hear these things in your normal daily life. This phenomena shuts down when your mirror gazing session is over.

The big difference between schizophrenia and psychic development is that no one is telling you what to do, and there is no sense of foreboding or paranoia. If you start hearing voices telling you to do something that you know is wrong, or telling you things that make you feel frightened, or you start thinking that people or things are out to get you, then that is a different matter; then you need professional help, but that sort of thing has nothing to do with mirror gazing.

Directing or controlling the session

Can you control the information that you receive? Well, yes to a certain degree, but not completely. This is the frustrating part for many people. What if you are hoping to get information about your business, but instead get guidance about your health? I have often heard it said that you don't always get what you want but you get what you need and this would be a good example of that.

Perhaps you want to see a particular loved one again but during the session someone else shows up. That is disappointing, but still a pretty wonderful experience. Why do some people seem to be able to come in more easily than others? I don't know for sure, but I suspect that it has more to do with the deceased person than it does with you. Some people just seem to be better able to manage it than others. Or perhaps the person you want to see is just too busy doing whatever it is they do on the other side to be able to show up on your timetable.

If you don't know where you are going any road will take you there

If you are not sure exactly what you want you might experience just about anything. This is not necessarily a bad thing. Like I said earlier, mirror gazing will give you what you need, but it might not be what you are expecting to get.

The key to getting what you want in your session is to set your intention.

Setting your intention

What do you hope to achieve in this session? The need to set your intention is so important to successful mirror gazing that I have gone into more detail about this later in the book, but basically it means to decide in advance exactly what you are hoping to achieve, being very clear about it, and giving the universe some advance warning so that, depending on your belief system, either your spirit beings or your brain have time to set things up.

Setting your intention for specific types of sessions

Easing grief by meeting and talking with deceased loved ones

I realize that having a mirror gazing experience with a deceased loved one does not replace their actual physical presence in your day to day life, but just knowing that they are okay goes a long way toward easing the grieving process.

If you have a particular loved one that you would like to contact, say so. Tell them out loud that you want to talk to them. Tell them what you want to talk about. Write them a letter saying that you miss them and that you would like to speak to them. You can also look at a picture or other small memento of them to help you focus your intention.

Lately my husband has taken to wearing his grandfather's St. Christopher medal, not because he believes that it will protect him from anything, but rather because it reminds him of his grandfather and seems to help him get through to his grandfather. When my husband does get through he and his grandfather mainly talk about family issues and my husband's career, exactly the sort of things they would have talked about when he was alive.

Meet spirit guides and angels

If your belief system includes a belief in spirit guides and angels then mirror gazing will allow you to meet them and get advice from them.

Similar to the spirit mentors example below, if you would like to meet with and develop a closer relationship with your spirit guides or angels simply make that your intention. Tell the universe what it is that you want to achieve, give them some time to set up the appointment and fit it into their schedule, and then don't be surprised when they show up.

Spirit mentors

What if it is a business problem that you want help with? Well think through the problem carefully and write down exactly what you are hoping to have happen. What exactly do you want to know? The action of writing it down helps you to clarify the problem. You might just find that when you do this you realize that you already know the answer. If you don't already know the answer, by doing this hours in advance of your mirror gazing session it gives your mind a chance to work on finding solutions to the problem.

Years ago I read Napoleon Hill's description of his experience with "make believe" spirit mentors. In his case he was an ambitious young man who had heard how having mentors would help his career. Since he didn't know any successful people who could give him advice he decided to have some imaginary mentors. He thought about famous figures in history that he would have liked to have known, people that he would like to be able to ask advice from. He made a list that included famous people like Abraham Lincoln, Benjamin Franklin, and George Washington and proceeded to pretend to ask for their advice. He would sit quietly, close his eyes and imagine himself talking to these men in a boardroom like setting. Before long he imagined them answering his questions, and the answers were really helpful. He received answers that were far beyond the scope of his personal experience. He began to fear for his sanity when he began hearing them discussing his questions amongst themselves, arguing at times, and he decided to stop the practice. But he soon realized that he missed their advice and began the procedure again.

For many years he was reluctant to tell anyone what he was doing because he thought that people would think he was crazy, and it wasn't until later in life that he revealed this secret. He did not know what to make of it, he never claimed to believe that he was actually speaking to these mentors. In other words he never claimed to be a Spiritualist, he never claimed to be speaking to the dead, but he acknowledged that the process was very helpful to him over the years.

As a Spiritualist I think that what he experienced was actual spirit contact, but it is not necessary for you to believe that in order to benefit from it. You can follow Napoleon Hill's practice with or without using the mirror. Simply think of someone who was extremely successful doing what ever it is that you want to do. In Napoleon Hill's case, one of the things he wanted to do was to publish his writings. Since Benjamin Franklin was a successful publisher Hill decided to ask Franklin for publishing advice. Obviously his advice was useful since Hill went on to publish numerous books that have sold millions and millions of copies and are still in print to this day.

So, what is the area that you want advice about? Is there someone in history that you think could help you? Set your intention to speak to that person, write out exactly what it is that you want to talk about. Set a time to get together with this spirit person when you know you will be sitting down to mirror gaze, and wait to see what happens. For best results treat this meeting as if you were having a meeting with a very busy successful person on the earth plane. Treat them with respect. Make sure to go into the meeting prepared, don't waste their time, know what you want from the session.

Looking for lost objects, or missing persons

Can't find your car keys or the TV remote? Ask the mirror for help. Do these things seem too insignificant to ask for? Well, big or small, in my experience it doesn't seem to make a difference. If you are meant to find it you will "see" where it is.

Only once have I tried to mirror gaze to find a missing person and the results that I got were very vague. There was nothing substantial that I could have gone to the authorities with. Why didn't it work this time? I don't know, perhaps it was me, maybe my head wasn't in the right place, or perhaps there is some reason why this person should not be found yet. At any rate, it has been several years now and this person is still missing.

Improve your creativity

Thomas Edison and Henry Ford both had their own methods of improving their creativity by tapping into the universal consciousness. Ford is quoted as claiming that he often came up with ideas in his sleep, that if he went to bed pondering a problem the solution would come to him in a dream.

In Edison's case it is claimed that he came up with his own method to tap into this sleep creativity. Apparently he kept a cot to sleep on in his office and he would ponder a problem and lie down on the cot holding handfuls of metal ball bearings. When he would drift off to sleep his grip on the ball bearings would loosen and the sound of the ball bearings falling into a metal pan on the floor would awaken him and he would jump up and write down the answer to the problem that was perplexing him.

The problem for most of us is that even if we get solutions to problems in our sleep, most of the time we can't remember the solutions upon arising. You can use mirror gazing to induce what some people refer to as lucid dreaming, or dreaming while in a wakened state. In this case you would clearly state the problem for which you are seeking a solution, write down what you know about the situation, and what the constraints or problems are, then inform the universe that you are looking for alternatives or solutions, and then sit down to mirror gaze. It is amazing how often the solution appears in the mirror.

Explore past lives

Are you curious about the concept of reincarnation? Do you think that you might have lived before? I don't see how it is possible to actually prove or disprove reincarnation, but it certainly is a fascinating topic to explore. Set your intention to view a past life and see what happens.

I have often heard people say that everyone who thinks they have lived before claims to have been someone famous. That is not my experience. The people in my classes who use the mirror to explore past lives usually experience very commonplace lives, not lives of great wealth or fame. This makes sense since these are the kind of lives that the majority of people throughout history have lived.

If you do use the mirror to explore a past life you will probably experience something that you can relate to your present life situation. Does this mean that you actually lived it before, or is it simply your mind creating a story that you can relate to? Or could you simply be viewing someone else's life? Does it really matter which it is as long as it works for you and helps you in your present situation?

Understand yourself better by delving into your subconscious

Why do I behave the way I do? We all have conditioned patterns and responses to stimulus. These patterns initially develop to help us cope, but often over time they can stop being a help and become a part of the problem. For example, perhaps you were a child in a very violent family. A logical defense mechanism would be to keep quiet and try to avoid drawing attention to yourself to limit the likelihood of getting beaten. This response makes perfect sense when you are a defenseless child, but does not necessarily benefit you in the business world when you are trying to promote a product or service. This is an extreme example but there might be other more subtle behavior patterns that are causing problems for you.

Make it your intention to ask the mirror why you behaved the way you did in a particular situation. You might be astonished to find yourself reliving an earlier event that set the pattern for your later behavior. Once you know why you do something you are better equipped to change the behavior.

Remote viewing

Remote viewing is the ability to "see" something with your mind even though you are not physically present. The U.S. military ran a research program called the Stargate Project to study remote viewing and determine if it could be used for espionage. They ultimately decided that, although it works, it is difficult to quantify and so it was difficult to justify spending the $20 million that they had spent on the program.

If it is your intention to visit somewhere without physically being there, it is a good idea to understand why you want to do this. What is your motive? Is it just a sightseeing trip, like a mini vacation? That is fine. As I write this I would rather be at the beach. But what if your motives are less than honorable? It is not a good idea to use this to spy on your ex, or on a business competitor. Take the time to think through your motives, then state what you want and why very clearly.

There are a number of ways of experiencing remote viewing. It could be like you are sitting in your chair watching images on a movie screen. Or it can feel like you are actually present, with your body, physically walking around the distant location. It can also feel like you are hovering over the place without a physical body. This last experience is often referred to as having an "out-of-body" experience.

See the past, present, and future

One of the really exciting aspects of mirror gazing is its ability to move us beyond the limitations of time. Do you want to witness a great event in history or see into the future? Keeping in mind that the future is not predetermined and is determined by our choices in the present, we can ask what the future will hold if we pursue a particular course of action today. This gives us the choice that if the outcome looks good then we can go with it, but if the outcome does not look appealing then we can simply make a change now that will result in a more desirable outcome in the future.

Visions can be different depending on what tool you use

Some people find that the visions they experience vary according to the particular tool they use. For example, I find that my visions are bigger and clearer when I look into a larger mirror. This makes no logical sense since the vision itself takes place in my mind, but I find it easier to see visions in a large mirror than in a small crystal. This is probably because my mind is telling me that I can see things better on a larger surface, kind of like watching a movie on a big high definition television versus watching the same movie on an iPod. Other people have better success with gazing at a particular piece of shiny jewelry, probably because there is some sort of emotional attachment to the piece. Other people seem to get better results with water.

I recommend starting with a black mirror because they are easy and inexpensive to make and then experimenting with other tools to see what kind of results you get later.

It gets easier with practice

Although some people in my classes have amazing experiences the first time they try it other people find that they get very little. But everyone finds that it gets easier over time. Getting yourself into the self hypnotic state of consciousness that is necessary for mirror gazing becomes easier each time you do it. As you continue to practice regularly, your mind learns how to enter the self-hypnotic state more easily and eventually you will find that you can enter this state immediately upon sitting down at your mirror.

Using mirror gazing to develop your psychic abilities

The discipline and focus that you develop through the practice of mirror gazing will help you to develop other psychic or mediumistic abilities. As you become more accustomed to "seeing" what is taking place in other dimensions of reality when mirror gazing it becomes easier to "see" when the mirror isn't present. We always have access to information from other information sources, and amazing things are taking place around us all the time, but most of the time we just don't notice because we aren't expecting it. Once your eyes are, in effect, opened through mirror gazing you will find it easier to tune in to these things the rest of the time.

Why is it that sometimes the information comes to us in metaphors and other times it is more clear and direct?

Oh how I wish I had a better answer to this question! I can't tell you how many times I have shouted at the universe to be more specific, more direct, to give me information in a way that can't possibly be misinterpreted. Is some higher power playing with us? I don't think so. The only explanation I can come up with is that sometimes the answers we want are just too complicated to be explained directly. I suspect that there is more going on than we are capable of understanding.

I am also convinced that some spirit communicators

are more adept than others. In other words, some spirit guides are easier for you to understand than others. Tell them that you don't understand, ask them to try explaining it to you some other way. If that doesn't work ask them to find someone else who can get through to you more easily. I remember back when I was in university I had a tutor to help me pass algebra, calculus and statistics courses. The first tutor and I just didn't connect. I simply wasn't getting it. I switched to another tutor and suddenly everything became much easier. So if your guide isn't easy to understand maybe you need to ask for a different one. I don't think you will be hurting their feelings.

I realize that this is not a completely satisfying answer, but it is the best I can come up with at this time. My best advice to you is to try mirror gazing and see what you experience.

The Legend of Narcissus

In Greek mythology Narcissus was a very proud young man who was renowned for his beauty. The gods decided to punish him for the disdainful way he treated other people by causing him to fall in love with an image he saw in a pool of water. He became obsessed with the beauty in the water. Not realizing that it was just his own reflection he was unable to pull himself away from the pool and wasted away to death.

J.K. Rowling used something similar to this in one of the Harry Potter books. After discovering the Mirror of Erised Harry begins spending long periods of time in front of the mirror until Professor Dumbledore hides it and warns Harry against looking for it again.

There are numerous other such stories throughout history, and they are a reminder to us that, although mirror gazing is exciting and very useful, we need to do everything in moderation.

Although it is great to get some help or to keep in touch with deceased loved ones on a regular basis, we have to guard against the real temptation to spend all of our time in communion with "the other side" and not spend enough time living in the present. We will be together with them on the other side soon enough, so make sure and really live this life while you are here.

Where do the visions come from? 4

Is mirror gazing dangerous?

Discussions about mirror gazing can elicit some strange responses in people. Most people are fascinated by it. Some because they think it will give you some sort of supernatural power, others because they think it is evil.

I particularly remember one conversation that I had with a woman who had heard that I would be teaching a class about mirror gazing. She was absolutely aghast that I would be endorsing something so "dangerous." I assured her that in my opinion, based on everything that I had witnessed and studied, mirror gazing was one of the safest of all methods of developing your psychic abilities and connecting with the other side.

"No, it is too dangerous. When you mirror gaze the mirror becomes a portal to other worlds, and if you aren't careful you won't be able to get back." she said.

"Oh really." I responded. "How do you know? Have

you ever personally witnessed a case where someone couldn't get back?"

"Oh yes, it happened to me." she replied.

Since the conversation was taking place on the porch of my cottage it was pretty obvious that she had managed to get back. I suspected that she had a vivid imagination and had been watching too many horror movies.

"Well you obviously managed to get back because you are standing here telling me about it. What happened?" I asked.

"It happened when I was about five years old. My grandmother had a big old mirror in her attic that she kept covered with a blanket. I had been warned not to touch it, but one day I went up and crawled under the blanket like a tent and looked into the mirror. The next thing I knew it was like the mirror opened up and engulfed me and I was trapped in a very scary world with strange creatures and I couldn't find my way back." she explained.

"Well what happened? You obviously got back somehow." I said.

"I don't know what happened. This strange creature was coming toward me and I screamed NO and suddenly I was back in the attic and the blanket was back in place covering the mirror. The experience terrified me and I had nightmares about it for years afterward." she said.

"So how long were you gone?" I asked. "Was your

family concerned about your disappearance?"

"Well, I guess I wasn't really gone for long, because no one else seemed to notice, but it felt like I had been trapped in the mirror for days." she replied.

I don't know if the incident actually took place or whether it was something that she had heard the adults around her talking about and she thought that it had happened to her, or whether it was something she had dreamed, I am simply relaying what she said to me.

She truly believed that it had happened, but obviously, whatever it was, even though she found the experience frightening, she was able to "come back" simply by saying NO and ending the session. If it did happen exactly the way she described it, I suspect that there were some things that she was going through in her life at that time, emotionally difficult things that as a five year old she was not able to understand.

Note: Since writing the above I told this story in a class and one of the students informed me that this woman's story was somewhat reminscent of the plot of an episode of the "Twilight Zone" television program from the 1960's. So it is possible that, although she actually believed that it had happened to her, she might have simply seen that episode on television as a child and been frightened by it.

But regardless of whether this event actually happened or if she imagined it, I think this story illustrates some points that I want to make about the "safety" of mirror gazing. First of all, it isn't a children's game. Even if the visions you experience are simply coming from your unconscious mind, you are opening up things that for some reason you had chosen to keep covered up. As adults we can choose to do this and then rationally analyze what we witnessed, but a child cannot do this. Young children possess a natural faculty for scrying, but as we grow older our logical, rational mind takes over and we no longer "see" as easily. In the past adults employed young children as scryers to take advantage of this natural ability, but this is no longer seen as appropriate. Occasionally, visions can be disturbing, even to an adult, so it would be unethical to subject a child to the consciousness altering techniques involved in mirror gazing.

You never know for sure what you are going to experience. For most of us this is part of what makes mirror gazing so fascinating. But if you are the type of person who wants to direct the action you might find this aspect of mirror gazing frustrating or unsatisfying.

Although the events are taking place in your mind, the presence of the speculum makes it appear that the events are taking place outside of you and so all you need to do to end it is to stop looking into the mirror, cover it with a cloth, or lay the mirror down and this will end the session.

However, people rarely experience anything that they would want to stop prematurely. The most common complaint is that the visions end sooner than they would like. The biggest challenge for most people is learning how to make the connection last longer.

So where do the visions come from?

Are the visions a form of direct communication from God? Well perhaps, depending on your beliefs about what God is. In my opinion, God is the word to describe the universal energy force that joins everything together, the universal consciousness, or super-conscious mind. So from that point of view I think that yes, the visions could be considered to be a way of tapping into this universal "God" consciousness.

Could they be communications from the spirits of departed loved ones? Absolutely! I am totally convinced that we are able to communicate with departed loved ones through the mirror. Of course, I am a Spiritualist and so I am already convinced that it is possible to communicate with spirits. I have had plenty of first hand experiences that have convinced me of this. You might be skeptical about this, and are simply trying to use the mirror as a form of meditation, or to develop your creativity, but I think that when you experience actually talking to a person in the mirror you will be inclined to believe that it is an actual person that you are talking to. Is it possible to prove it to someone else's satisfaction, perhaps not, but does convincing someone else really matter as long as what you experienced was satisfying for you?

What about messages from spirit guides or angels? Yes, if your belief system includes spirit guides and angels then I think it is possible to communicate with them through the mirror. Is it possible to "prove" that you are communicating with one of these spirit beings? That is a tough one. Personally I am convinced that spirit guides exist, but I can't see how it can be proven. Yes, you can get good information and facts that you were previously unaware of, but how can you prove that it came from an angel or a spirit guide and not from your unconscious mind or from tapping into the universal consciousness?

If you ask an evangelical Christian they would probably tell you that the visions in the mirror are from Satan; that they are demonic, which leads me to the next topic.

Contradictions in Christianity & Judaism

The Bible contains many contradictory passages regarding divination and attempting to contact the deceased. For example, Deuteronomy 18:10-11 seems to say very clearly that you should not perform divination (fortune telling) or attempt to call upon the dead.

> *10 There shall not be found among you any one that maketh his son or his daughter to pass through the fire, or that useth divination, or an observer of times, or an enchanter, or a witch.*
>
> *11 Or a charmer, or a consulter with familiar spirits, or a wizard, or a necromancer.*

Exodus 22:18 very clearly states, *"Thou shalt not suffer a witch to live."*

Leviticus 19:3, 20:6, and 20:27 also clearly indicate that one should not attempt divination or contact with the deceased.

Galatians 5:20 lists witchcraft as one of the sins that Christians need to renounce.

However, Exodus 28:30 refers to the Urim and Thummin which were objects the priests used for divination, and Genesis 44:5 refers to the silver cup that Joseph used for scrying and dream interpretation.

In Daniel chapter 5 we read that Daniel was the supervisor of magicians, astrologers, and soothsayers in King Belshazzar's court, and gives an account of what happened when he was asked to interpret a disturbing vision that the king had seen.

So it would appear to me that the Bible is advocating a two-tiered system where only priests and God's chosen ones are allowed to practice divination, contact the deceased, and get direct guidance, and that the rest of us are prohibited. One of the big problems with this is that it leaves the rest of us dependent on the chosen few. This leaves us vulnerable to manipulation and fraud. For more of my thoughts on this subject refer to my book *"Pious Fraud: How religion has evolved throughout history."* ISBN 978-1-926826-02-8.

The subconscious or unconscious mind

The terms subconscious mind and unconscious mind are often used interchangeably, perhaps not completely accurately, but for our purposes this is fine. Basically we are referring to information that we "know" but are not consciously aware of. Such as information that we learned somewhere in the past, but have filed away and have forgotten, or information that we have suppressed for some reason, often because remembering it elicits some sort of unpleasant emotion.

The term "unconscious mind" is used in psychoanalysis to describe thoughts that we are not able to access directly through ordinary introspection. Sigmund Freud called the unconscious mind a repository for socially unacceptable ideas, desires, or painful emotions that we choose not to remember.

> DISCLAIMER: Mirror gazing can be used as a psychoanalytic tool to help unlock suppressed trauma, but this is not necessarily a do-it-yourself project. If you are experiencing emotional or psychological problems you might consider seeking professional help.

Freud used his psychoanalytic theories about the unconscious mind to explain certain kinds of neurotic behavior, but we can have information or memories locked up in our unconscious mind for other reasons besides trauma, and these unconscious thoughts do not necessarily have to cause neurotic behavior.

Without the unconscious mind actively at work we would be unable to do more than one thing at a time. The unconscious mind is like a powerful computer processing millions of pieces of data every second to enable us to perform the ordinary tasks of our lives.

Our unconscious mind is hard at work while we talk on the phone and file our nails or pet the dog. If we had to devote our conscious attention to every activity we could only do one thing at a time.

Remember what it was like when you first were learning

how to drive a car, the simple act of turning on the car radio while driving was almost more than you could handle, and yet after years of driving who has not experienced pulling up at your destination and realizing that you didn't remember part of the trip. Repetition helps to firmly establish something in your unconscious mind. Learning to play a musical instrument is an example of this.

The unconscious mind is sometimes the source of thoughts that appear out of the blue for no apparent reason. Our unconscious mind can work on solutions to problems without our being aware of it. Everyone has had the experience of being unable to think of a solution to a problem (or in my case, trying unsuccessfully to remember a name) and giving up only to have the answer flash into your mind days later for no apparent reason.

The unconscious mind is also believed to be the source of our night time dreams, which are often our mind's way of processing confusing emotions and experiences.

Making sense out of senseless situations

Like dream analysis, mirror gazing can be used as a method of making sense of otherwise senseless experiences. I experienced this very vividly on one particular occasion.

I was sitting in a hotel lobby with a group of friends listening as someone in the group related a funny story. We were all enjoying the experience, I was smiling and others in the group were laughing out loud, when a man that I knew only casually, and had previously had no significant interchanges with, suddenly walked into the room and singled me out. He began to berate me loudly and blamed me, unfairly, for the noise which he claimed had disturbed his sleep.

I was astounded. From my perspective I had been sitting there quietly, part of a large group of people in a public place. I certainly did not feel that I deserved the verbal abuse that was heaped on me. He obviously wasn't behaving rationally and I didn't see any point in arguing with him so I left and went home, at which point he turned on someone else in the group. I walked home feeling hurt, embarrassed and angry and I was totally at a loss to explain what had happened and why.

Since I am a believer in taking personal responsibility for everything that happens in my life I tried to logically analyze why this event had happened. What was the lesson in it for me, how could I benefit from the experience? I couldn't figure it out, so that night before getting into bed I asked for an explanation of why the event happened (depending on your perspective you might say I prayed for an answer). I expected an event to take place that would explain it, or perhaps a dream, or even just to have an idea pop into my head that would explain the event, but what happened was even more fascinating.

I went to bed and tossed and turned for a while. Finally I got up and sat on the edge of the bed. My husband was sound asleep so I didn't want to turn the light on. I just sat there for a few minutes in the dark room thinking about the upsetting event. There was a regular mirror on the dresser in front of the bed, not a black mirror, just a regular bedroom mirror. I wasn't intentionally attempting to scry, I just happened to be sitting there and I noticed the familiar cloud patterns beginning to form on the mirror. Then suddenly it was as though I was watching a movie. It was a replay of an actual event that had happened a few days previously. It wasn't a significant event and I had completely forgotten about it until I saw it playing out in the mirror. I watched as the man who had berated me walked past my husband. I heard my husband make a joke, trying to be pleasant, certainly not intending to offend the other man, and I saw the man smile back. It seemed like a completely innocuous interchange, but I realized at that moment that, although the man smiled, he had actually misinterpreted the meaning, the intention, of my husband's comments and was upset. He was apparently upset about lots of things in his life, not just the comment my husband made. Obviously he had stewed on it for a few days and when the situation presented itself he took out all of his anger and frustration on me.

I was still upset by the incident, but now I could see why it happened, and I could understand the man's frustration. Seeing the incident played out in the mirror didn't change what happened, but it certainly has enabled me to feel compassion for him.

Where did the vision come from? Well obviously it came from my unconscious mind. It was a memory of an event that had previously taken place that I had simply forgotten. I think that my guides brought it to my attention when I asked for an answer, however I realize that I can't prove that to anyone else's satisfaction.

It is also possible that my unconscious mind was searching for an answer to my question and came up with this memory as an explanation. The mirror was a convenient and clear way of showing me the memory.

Carl Jung and the collective unconscious

Carl Jung developed Freud's concept regarding the unconscious mind even further. He divided the unconscious into two parts: the personal unconscious and the collective unconscious. The personal unconscious is made up of all the memories that were once part of our own experience but have since been forgotten or suppressed, while the collective unconscious could be described as all of the accumulated memories and archetypal experiences of everyone throughout history.

Our unconscious mind seems to be able to tap into these universal memories and experiences to make sense of our world. Many scholars would claim that this is an oversimplification of the concept but I think it is adequate for our purposes.

The super-conscious mind

Many people believe that there is a super-conscious mind or energy power that, similar to Jung's "collective unconscious," contains the answers to all of life's problems. You could call this God, or you could think of it as the reservoir of all knowledge. Some people talk about the Akashic Records which are supposed to contain everything that has happened in the past as well as everything that will happen in the future. Regardless of what we call it, or how extensive this reservoir of knowledge actually is, our mind is the powerful antenna that enables us to tap into it.

Everyone has had the experience of getting a really good idea, perhaps an idea for a story or an invention, but for whatever reason you do nothing with the idea and then a little while later someone else comes up with the same idea and runs with it. Did they somehow steal your idea? No, I don't think so. I think that ideas are floating around us all the time in the collective unconscious or super-conscious mind, and it is up to us to seize the idea and run with it or someone else will.

Mirror gazing is one way of tapping into this reservoir of ideas.

Archetypes - a picture is worth a thousand words

When we sit down at the mirror to scry, we are sending a message to our unconscious mind that we are looking for information that is beyond the reach of our conscious awareness.

Our consciousness is made up of sensory impressions. We understand our world through our senses: we see, hear, touch, taste, feel, and smell. This is why babies put everything into their mouths, they are learning about things through the use of their senses.

Sometimes the information from our unconscious comes to us in the form of a movie playing out on the screen of the mirror, as it did in the case I just described. Sometimes it comes in sounds, smell, or tastes, but many times the information comes in the form of still pictures. I realize that it is hard to understand how something like a taste, a smell, or a sound can be illustrated on a mirror. I think the only way to really understand this is to experience it for yourself.

There is an old saying that a picture is worth a thousand words. We can see a picture and suddenly understand far more than just the surface meaning of the picture. This is because of what Jung described as "archetypes" which are universal symbols that are understood across cultures. Sometimes the picture that we see in the mirror represents an actual situation or event, while other times it is an archetypical symbol. Tarot cards are an example of a divination system based on archetypical symbols that most people are able to instinctively understand.

Time travel

Sometimes when we are scrying we are looking for answers from the past, other times we want to know something that will take place in the future, so in effect we are attempting to use the mirror to travel through time. Are we actually traveling through time? I can't prove it, but it certainly feels that way when you are experiencing it.

One of the students in my class had a fascinating encounter with his grandmother in the mirror. We had done a group meditation and as he sat quietly looking into the mirror his grandmother appeared. She looked exactly as he had remembered her before she passed over. After some greetings, he asked her about her early life, about events that had taken place before he was born; things he had never thought to ask her about when she was alive. Instantly he found himself moving through a rapid series of places and events. He found himself in her first apartment where she was a young married woman who had recently immigrated to the United States.

He went further back and found himself in a tiny cabin on the ship that she had travelled on. Then further back he was in her childhood home in Poland. He felt like he was actually there with her in each of these places at these earlier times. He smelled the aromas, he felt the temperature, and he heard the sounds. In his mind he was convinced that he had travelled through time with her.

Could he prove it? No, but he was convinced. For him time was distorted, he felt like he had been several hours in the mirror when in fact he was only sitting there for 20 minutes during the class, and obviously his body had never left his chair.

Layers of reality

Have you ever seen an anatomy chart that has transparent layers that show the different parts of the human body? The kind where you can lift off each layer and you can see what is under it? Well I think that our reality is like that. I think there are layers and layers of reality one on top of the other, like the layers of an onion. What we usually see is just the layer of reality that we are living in at the moment, but I think that other layers of reality exist at the same time in the same place. Other entities/beings might possibly be living their lives in the same place and at the same time as we are but we don't see them.

Everything is energy, and everything vibrates at its own rate or speed. Those who have passed on to spirit still exist, but they are not tied down to physical bodies so it is believed that they vibrate at a higher/faster level than we in the physical world do. So in Spiritualism we talk about "raising the vibration" which means that we attempt to raise our energy level closer to theirs in order to make contact. It is believed that they in turn must slow their vibration rate in order to meet us in an area between the two worlds. This is sometimes referred to as the "astral plane," the "ethereal plane," or "the middle realm."

The "middle realm"

The "middle realm" could be thought of as sort of a neutral area half way between our level of reality and that of the spirit world. It is a place where it is safe for us to meet. We haven't actually crossed over into death, and they haven't actually come back to life. This middle realm isn't really a physical place but a mental place that we create in our mind.

The mirror can create sort of a doorway to this middle realm. Mirror gazing is not the only way to create the doorway. Many people are able to slip back and forth into this middle realm without any tools, simply by creating the doorway in their mind. But the mirror is a handy tool for developing this ability.

Performing a ritual that you always follow when attempting to link to the spirit world is another way of creating a doorway or link. That is why you sometimes see mediums doing seemingly odd things as they begin to connect to spirit. One man I know always begins with a sing-songish prayer before he begins. This used to irritate me until I understood that this was his way of signalling to his mind that it is time to slide into the middle realm. Another woman I know turns to one side and sort of takes a step as a signal to her mind of her intention to connect with spirit.

Creating your own ritual is so important that I have devoted an entire chapter to it later in this book.

Do we need protection from malevolent entities or evil spirits?

Mirror gazing is the safest method of attempting to develop your psychic abilities because the speculum (the mirror) provides a psychological or perceptual filter between us and anything outside of us that we might perceive as threatening. Any time that something does not feel pleasant, any time that we want to end the session we simply have to decide to end the session and either flip the mirror over or cover it with a cloth. Also, you can choose to dispose of the mirror, break it and throw it in the garbage and you have effectively destroyed the doorway to the other world that you had created.

In addition, if we follow a ritual which involves starting off the session by setting our intention that everything that occurs will be for the highest and the best then as far as I am concerned you are pretty well covered. Or if you have other religious beliefs and ask a particular entity (like Jesus or angels for example) for protection before you start then that would do it for you as well.

DISCLAIMER: If you truly believe that you are vulnerable to malevolent entities like demons then you should not attempt ANY form of psychic development.

I do not feel that it is necessary, but many people who mirror gaze follow the Wiccan practice of casting a circle of salt around them for protection.

Do I believe that negative entities exist? Yes, I think that it is likely that there are unpleasant, evil, confused, lower vibrating, or less evolved energies around us all the time. Nasty people exist on the earth plane, why wouldn't they exist on the ethereal plane as well. Am I afraid of them? No, not at all, I think we attract to ourselves things that are consistent with, or similar to, our own energy. Much of the time we experience what we expect to experience, and I choose not to expect to experience dangerous or unpleasant experiences unless it is in my best interest to do so.

Trickster spirits

Throughout history, in almost every culture that I am aware of, people have believed that there are "trickster" spirits which are entities that seem to take great delight in confusing people and causing plans to go awry. It is almost inevitable that at some point you will run across such spirits as you embark on your psychic development.

If, in your mirror gazing, you encounter an entity who claims to be some particular person, but for some reason it just doesn't feel right then go with your instinct. Remember, you control the experience, you do not have to do anything that any spirit entity tells you to do.

Use your common sense. As we often say in Spiritualism, if your uncle Joe was not someone you would go to for advice while he was alive, just because he has now crossed over to the spirit world does not mean that he has suddenly become wise. By the same token, just because some entity shows up in your mirror it doesn't mean that you should follow their advice.

Whatever you send out you will get back

While I believe that mirror gazing and spirit contact is generally very safe, a lot depends on your intention. If your intention when mirror gazing is not for the highest and best, if you are attempting to do something unethical, then I think you are opening yourself up to evil or unpleasantness.

For example if you are using mirror gazing to get an unfair advantage over someone else, or if you are using the mirror to attempt to snoop in areas that are not your concern (like remote viewing in your neighbor's house without their consent) then it is likely that something similarly unpleasant will happen to you, not necessarily immediately, but eventually you will pay for your behavior. What goes around comes around.

Do you have to "believe" in order for it to work?

No, it is not necessary to "believe" in anything for mirror gazing to work for you. It helps if you have a sense of positive expectancy, in other words if you expect that something interesting will happen, but many people are total skeptics when they first try it and still have astounding experiences.

The important thing is that you acknowledge everything that is taking place. I have found that if you simply acknowledge whatever you are noticing, for example, say to yourself that the mirror seems to be getting darker, or lighter then things will progress rapidly from there. Usually you will then see cloud shapes develop and then something will form out of the clouds. However, if you don't acknowledge what is happening then often it just seems to stall there.

If something exciting happen does happen in your mirror, for example if you meet with your grandmother, or you travel to an exotic land, you do not have to believe that it actually happened. The experience is yours alone, you are welcome to attribute it to your over-active imagination if you choose.

Preparing your tools

As we saw earlier in this book, scrying can be done using a variety of instruments from something as elaborate as an expensive beryl crystal ball to something as simple as a polished fingernail.

While it is true that the magic is in you, not in the tool, it is important to remember that your scrying tool, whatever tool you choose, is not a toy or a decoration for your home.

What you perceive in the spirit or astral world is created within your own mind. The speculum is simply the screen upon which your mind projects the information. But, if you treat your speculum with respect and treat it as though it possesses a power of its own then it will indeed have power in your mind. If you handle it carelessly and leave it out for anyone to touch or play with then it will not hold much importance in your mind, and you will not be able to get the best results from it.

Make your own inexpensive scrying mirror

It is possible to buy expensive black glass or polished stone mirrors for scrying, but in my classes the students use simple black mirrors that I make from inexpensive picture frames. These work extremely well and are very easy to make. Some of the most incredible visions have resulted from the use of these simple scrying mirrors.

Here is the method I use for making them:

1) Gather your materials:

• Get an inexpensive **8" by 10" picture frame** with glass, not plastic. Although the picture on the cover of this book shows an elaborate, ornate mirror frame, ideally it should be a plain black wooden frame since elaborate, ornate frames can be distracting, especially at first. Find one that has a stand on the back so that it will be able to stand up on the table in front of you when in use. Do not try to use a regular mirror since we want to make the back of the glass black, not silver the way mirrors usually are.

• A small bottle of flat **black acrylic craft paint**. This can be found in the craft department of discount stores. Any brand is fine. A small 2 oz./59 ml. bottle is enough to do several mirrors.

• A flat (not round) **paint brush** to smooth the paint out on the surface of the glass.

• An 8" by 10" piece of **black construction paper**.

• **Newspaper** to protect your work area, and **paper towels** for clean up.

Any inexpensive free-standing black picture frame will work

Any brand of flat black acrylic craft paint will do

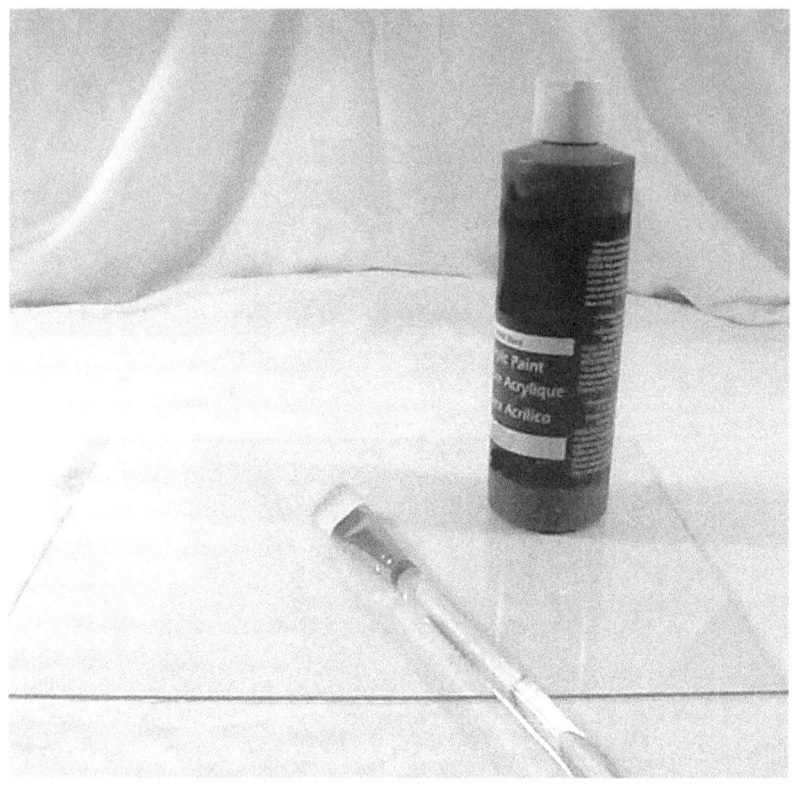

2) Prepare your work area:

• Lay out some newspaper over the table where you will be working.

• Wear something that you can get paint on. Most acrylic paint will wash out if you wash it immediately, but if it has even a few moments to set your clothing will be permanently marred. Black is particularly permanent.

3) Prepare the picture frame:

• Open up the picture frame and take out and discard any mat piece or packaging that is inside.

• Carefully remove the glass from the frame and set it on the newspaper. Be careful, the edges of the glass are sharp.

• Set the picture frame and backing aside to be assembled again later after everything has dried.

4) Paint the back of the glass:

• Pour out some of the black craft paint onto the back of the glass. Use the brush to smooth a thick coat of paint out to the edges of the glass. Don't be too fiddly with this, just try to let the paint flow out across the glass. Don't worry if the first coat isn't perfect, it will probably require several coats.

• **Let it dry thoroughly before you give it another coat**. You will find that the paint just sort of sits on the glass, it does not penetrate the glass so be very careful when you apply the second and any subsequent layers of paint or you will cause ripples in the underlying layers. Pour a small amount of paint onto the glass and very gently spread it out with the brush, try not to rub the earlier dried paint with the brush or you could cause it to lift off and ripple.

• If for some reason you mess it up completely and have too many ripples you can always just soak the painted glass in water before it has completely cured, and the dried paint will lift and peel off and you can start over.

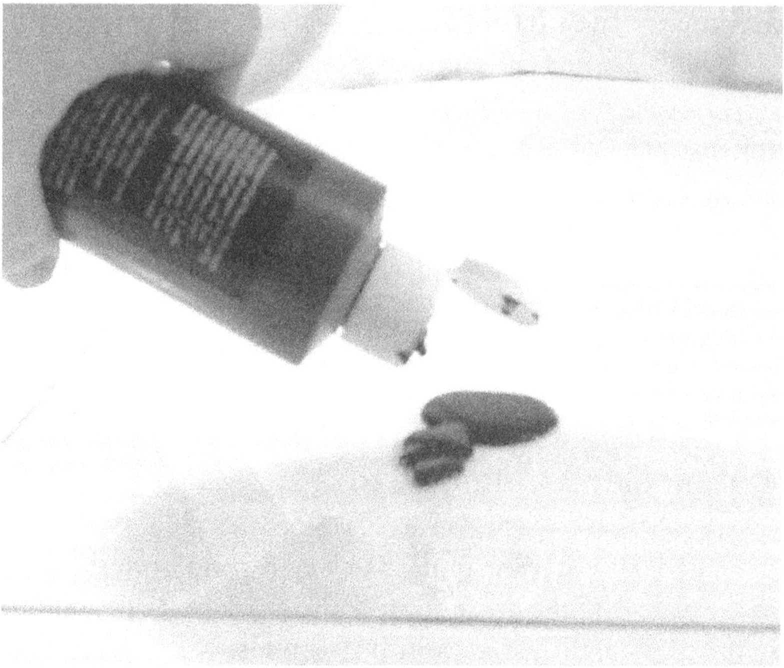

Pour the paint onto the back of the glass and then drag it to the edges with the paint brush.

• Once the paint is thoroughly dry hold the glass up to the light and look for areas that are missing paint. It will never look absolutely perfect because of the nature of painting on glass, but as long as there are no large unpainted areas it will appear solid when you put the glass back in the frame. The black construction paper will help to compensate for some unevenness in the paint.

• Wash your brush carefully with dish soap and warm water before the paint dries.

The completed scrying mirror

5) Put the frame back together.

• Place the 8" by 10" piece of black construction paper behind the glass inside the frame. This gives the glass a more even appearance, and makes the glass seem deeper. I have tried using black construction paper alone, without the paint, but I don't find that you get as nice or as deep a dark appearance without the paint.

6) Polish up the front of the mirror with a paper towel and some glass cleaner or vinegar to take off any fingerprints and smudges and your scrying mirror is ready to use.

Consecrating your mirror

People use all sorts of methods to "consecrate" or bless their mirror before use. Some of the methods include setting it up on a window ledge under moonlight, placing it outside in the sunshine, or placing a small dish of rock salt in front of it overnight.

Do you need to consecrate or cleanse the mirror to remove any negative energies before you use it? Well, probably not, but personally, I choose to smudge any new mirror before using it, not that I think that there might be any negative energies attached to it, but simply to "bless" the mirror and remind myself that the mirror is special. To smudge the mirror I take a smudge stick, which is a clump of sage or sweetgrass tied together, and light it and sweep the smoke over the mirror. This creates a sort of smoke bath over the mirror to cleanse it of any residual energies from previous use.

When teaching my classes I use the same mirrors over

and over again with new students so before the class I smudge each of the mirrors to provide a clean slate for the new user, not because the previous users energy is negative, but just in case the residual energy left by the previous user might result in confusing images for the next person using the mirror.

The magic is in the intention, not in the smoke itself. The smoke is simply a visual representation of our intention to bless the mirror.

I think that even the act of polishing your mirror with a paper towel and vinegar, done with the correct attitude, with the intention of blessing the mirror, is sufficient to consecrate it.

Setting up your scrying location

Setting up an area dedicated to meditation and mirror gazing has always proven to be a challenge for me. We live in a small apartment, and finding a quiet, private space to set things up is an ongoing problem. Every space in our apartment serves multiple purposes, so simply the act of sitting in a particular chair is not enough to signal to my mind that I am ready to meditate. Instead, I keep my tools in a drawer and bring them out when I am ready to "sit." For more about this see the chapter on the importance of ritual in mirror gazing.

Keep your tools covered when not in use

As I mentioned earlier, your scrying tools are not toys or decorations for your home. Keep them covered when they are not in use. Even if you have a room with a locking door that is dedicated solely to mirror gazing you should cover your mirror with a cloth when not in use. Removing the cover becomes the signal to your mind, to your unconscious, that you are looking for information that is not generally accessible to your conscious mind.

Scrying in water

Some of the most famous scryers in history used a bowl of water to scry. I have a black stone scrying bowl that is polished inside and when filled with water it gives the illusion of endless depth, as though you are peering into an abyss. I also have a black glass bowl that produces a similar effect. Some people use a clear glass bowl filled with a dark colored liquid like grape juice.

Some people scry using a wine glass filled with water. Into the water they drop a few drops of dark food coloring and let it gradually dissipate into the water. Watching the color swirl into the clear water is the trigger for them that lets their mind know that they are ready to begin scrying.

It is even possible to scry with a glass of red wine. Sitting quietly on a comfortable chair, on a cold winter night, in a darkened room, with a fire going in the fireplace, sipping a large glass of red wine is almost guaranteed to put a person into the kind of altered state that encourages visions, assuming that you are drinking only 1 or 2 glasses. Beyond that you lose the necessary concentration to do it effectively.

Mesmerism and magnetic energy

Appendix B of this book contains an abridgement of the book "Crystal Gazing and Clairvoyance" by John Melville. In it you will see that during the 1700's and 1800's, before we understood what we now know about self hypnotic trance states, it was believed that a magnetic force was involved in clairvoyance and visions.

To simplify a complex theory, basically it was thought that the chemical makeup of a beryl crystal had the ability to draw in or attract the unseen world, and that when a person focused their eyes on the crystal a stream of "magnetism" went from the eyes to the crystal and drew into the person's mind the images that had been concentrated and magnified by the crystal. Hence, beryl crystal was considered to be the most desirable scrying tool, followed by quartz crystal.

Crystal balls

Crystal balls come in varying sizes from small ½ inch balls that can hang on a chain around your neck to huge, wildly expensive 10 inch or greater sized balls. It is not necessary to spend thousands of dollars on a crystal ball for scrying. Many people still believe that crystal magnifies the psychic energy but I have not found that to be the case. I have found that a piece of glass can work as well as a crystal (of course I should probably qualify this statement by admitting that I have never had the opportunity to use a very large, very expensive clear beryl crystal, maybe if I did I would change my tune, but I doubt it).

Also, although I do happen to own a 3 inch clear quartz crystal ball, and several smaller colored quartz crystal balls, as well as numerous glass balls in varying sizes, I find that I prefer the larger expanse of surface that an inexpensive glass picture frame provides. The size of the surface really doesn't matter once the vision gets going, because the vision tends to expand beyond the size of the tool, but initially, when the vision is just beginning, I find it easier to see the cloud formations beginning on the larger dark expanse of the mirror than on the smaller surface of a crystal ball.

Choosing a crystal ball

There is an old saying that the crystal ball chooses its user, well actually it goes more like "the crystal chooses the witch" but many people erroneously believe the witch connotation to be negative or indicative of black magic. What this really means is that if you want a crystal ball there is probably one out there whose energy resonates with yours, or in other words one ball will "feel" better to you than another. Also, it might find its way into your possession in some unusual fashion. For example it might be given to you unexpectedly, or you will find it for sale in an unusual location for a very reasonable price (I heard of one large quartz crystal ball winding up in a clothing bin at a Goodwill store!), or the money to purchase one will come to you in an unusual manner.

Clear crystal or colored crystal?

Whether to choose a clear crystal, a colored or smoky crystal, or one that contains internal flaws or blemishes is a matter of personal preference. Clear crystals which contain no internal flaws are very rare and therefore very expensive, but many people like them because they are like a clean slate upon which to project the vision, and many people believe that they work best to magnify the psychic energy.

As I mentioned previously, I have never noticed a

magnification of the psychic energy through the use of a clear quartz ball, but I have noticed that quartz crystals definitely give off a different energy in my hand when holding one. In fact, that is pretty much the only way I can tell the difference between my 3 inch clear quartz crystal ball and a 3 inch glass ball that I have which was made in China and was sold as an ornament in a Target store for $3.

Other people prefer to use crystals that have internal flaws which give your eyes and conscious mind something to focus on while your unconscious mind gets ready to start the show.

Some people like to use particular colors for different purposes. For example, you might want to use an amethyst crystal for its calming soothing energy, or a rose quartz crystal if you are inquiring about romantic matters. However, I don't think this is necessary.

Using a crystal ball

When many people first hear about scrying they imagine an old Gypsy woman leaning over a crystal ball. The crystal ball sits on a stand and she peers into it. However most people who use crystal balls for scrying sit the ball on a small cushion and surround the ball with black cloth, either silk or velvet, to create a dark depth inside the crystal with no reflections from the room. It then becomes similar to looking into a dark pool of water.

If you want to begin using a crystal ball you might want to get a small wooden box just the right size to hold your crystal ball. Line the box, including the hinged lid, with black fabric, either silk or velvet. The lid opens to reveal the ball inside, and the black fabric creates a black background. If you place a piece of black fabric over your head and over the box to create a tent, it helps concentrate the energy and creates an ideal setting for scrying during the day time. I have tried to do it this way, but my major difficulty with this is that it feels too claustrophobic for me. Also, leaning over the ball does not feel comfortable for me. I prefer to lean back and relax in my chair and gaze at an expanse of black mirror. To overcome these difficulties I am experimenting with using a curtained off "cabinet" like they used in the old days of Spiritualism for creating a small darkened area.

Building a modern psychomanteum

A polished rock or a $4 picture frame sitting on your kitchen table is all that you really need to get started mirror gazing, but it is inevitable that as time goes on, if you really get into this, you will probably want something more elaborate.

In his book *"Reunions,"* Dr. Raymond Moody talks about building a modern day psychomanteum, or apparition booth.

The word psychomanteum dates back to ancient Greece, where there was a facility set up in the city of Ephyra where people would go to gaze into a pool of water with the intention of seeing visions of their dead loved ones. The supplicants would wait in complete darkness before taking their turn walking through a darkened hallway into the apparition chamber. In the chamber there was a bronze cauldron surrounded by a banister where people would gaze into the cauldron. The room was designed with very limited lighting which was provided by flickering candle light. This flickering low light helped to induce the trance state.

You can create your own modern psychomanteum if you have a space that you can dedicate exclusively to this. The idea is to set up a space that takes you away from your normal day to day routine.

The ideal situation would be if you had a large property with a small building in the back corner of your garden where you would go only to scry. The interior could be painted in a dark flat, not glossy paint and you could furnish it with a huge mirror, a comfortable chair, strategically placed candles in candle holders, a few crystals, a bowl of water on a shelf, and have your meditation music ready to go. If desired, you could decorate it with some religious symbolism to make you feel closer to your God, and the pathway leading up to it would be lined with flowers. No telephones allowed, and no clocks, nothing to connect you with your day-to-day stresses.

A nice dream, however, few of us have such a luxury. What you would absolutely need is a small area that you could devote exclusively to scrying. A large closet would work if it was big enough for you to safely burn a candle, or have an electric candle plugged in, and if there was adequate ventilation and enough room for you to sit comfortably in front of the mirror. You could also set up in a corner of your basement.

The main challenge, if you live with other people, is to find a way to sit peacefully in your psychomanteum without being drawn into the life being lived in the rest of the house. Evening is an ideal time to scry, so perhaps you could just plan your scrying time when your family members are asleep.

Setting up your mirror

If you are creating your own psychomanteum and are mounting a scrying mirror on the wall there are a few points that you will want to keep in mind.

1) If possible do not place the mirror flat on the wall. Instead, mount the mirror so that the bottom of the mirror is out from the wall at perhaps a 30 degree angle. You can mount some wood on the wall at the bottom of the mirror to hold it at the correct angle. Ths will probably require some trial and error to get it at exactly the right angle.

Example of mounting a mirror on a wall at an angle of approx. 30 degrees

You could also use a mirror on a floor stand if you take out the original mirror and replace it with black glass. The floor stand would make it easy for you to adjust the mirror to the ideal angle for you.

2) Regarding the chair, find one that will allow you to recline back at a 30% angle. Position it so that you are looking into the mirror but are not looking at your reflection.

3) Have a cloth cover for your mirror for when it is not in use. Find something dark, it doesn't have to be black. A fabric with a beautiful pattern that makes you feel good is ideal. This helps to reinforce the idea that this mirror is special.

4) Have a spot to place your candles or electric candles behind you and off to the sides. Have the candles shaded so that you get the trance inducing benefit of the flickering light, but the light is not shining in your eyes or reflecting in the mirror.

5) Have a shelf or small table upon which you set a small bowl of fresh water and perhaps some fresh flowers.

Basically, you want to create a comfortable space where you can see into the black depth of the mirror but not be looking at your own reflection. You want to be able to relax back into the chair but not be so comfortable that you fall off to sleep. You want to create a beautiful, peaceful, private spot that makes it easy for you to go into a trance state, and invites spirit contact.

Ideal angle for mirror and chair

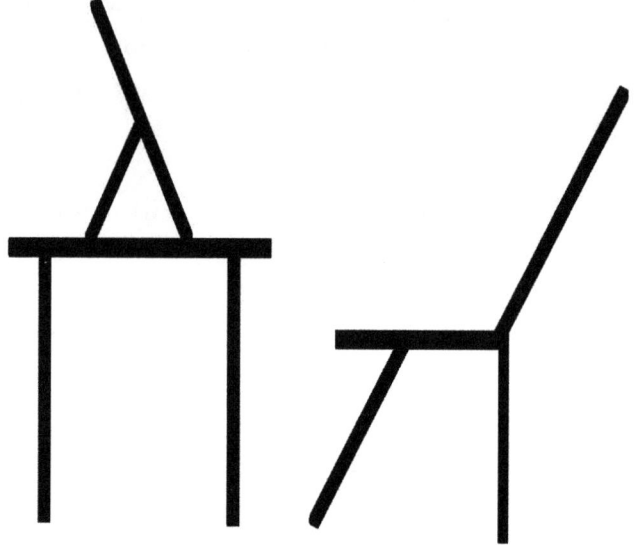

The importance of ritual   6

Since the visions actually take place only in our mind, rather than in the mirror, creating the proper state of mind is an important factor in successful mirror gazing. As I mentioned earlier, this state of mind is sometimes referred to as the "astral" or "etheral plane" to differentiate it from an actual physical place. So, you could think of a mirror gazing ritual as an on-off switch for the part of your mind that creates this "astral plane."

A ritual is any repetitive act that helps to create an atmosphere or mood that allows the mind to detach from the day to day cares of the world and tune into the mysteries of the universe. In other words, the primary purpose of ritual is to put yourself into the right frame of mind. The mind rebels against discipline, so everything that you can do to help condition your mind is a valuable exercise.

Some people perform very elaborate rituals believing that they are absolutely necessary for successful mirror gazing, while other people place no emphasis on ritual at all, and both of these groups are successful. In the past I leaned away from elaborate rituals, believing that simply setting your intention was enough; however, over time I have come to a greater appreciation of the value of ritual in spiritual work.

A simple ritual

An adequate ritual can be as simple as setting up your mirror, sitting in the same chair facing the same direction, setting up your tools in the same manner, lighting a candle, and asking for a vision (you might consider this to be "praying" depending on your religious belief system). By following even a simple ritual like this you are telling your mind, as well as the spirit world, that you are prepared to receive visions.

The following are some examples of other actions that you might want to incorporate in your own personal mirror gazing ritual:

A clean room

Everyone feels more comfortable in a clean room. Take a moment to tidy the area where you are going to scry. Dust the table top, sweep the floor. You are, in effect, inviting guests into your mirror gazing space so prepare accordingly.

Throughout history witches were often depicted with a broom. This is nothing sinister or mysterious, it simply represents cleaning away anything that we don't need. Wiccans often perform a ritual sweep with a broom or besom before sitting down to scry to symbolize cleaning away the old and opening up your mind to new possibilities. If you want you can start and finish your sweeping near a door so that when you are finished sweeping any negative energy can be symbolically swept outside of the room.

Asperging is another method of ritually cleansing a space. The word asperging means to sprinkle a liquid, usually some form of consecrated or "holy" water around the area. Some people use other liquids such as wine or oil to sprinkle around the area, but not in my house!

Clean clothes

You might want to have a special piece of clothing such as a robe or a shawl that is reserved exclusively for mirror gazing and never worn at any other time. Putting on this piece of clothing assists in triggering the proper mental state.

If you choose to use an item of ritual clothing it needs to be kept clean, treated with respect, and stored separately from your everyday clothing. A special piece of jewelry, or a head covering would also work.

A clean body

Ritual cleansing can be as simple as washing your hands. In many Spiritualist Churches, prior to doing hands-on healing, the healers rinse their hands in water. Since this rinsing is not as involved as that of a surgeon prepping for surgery this act is more for symbolic purposes than for hygienic purposes. It is a reminder that you are removing the energy of the day, or of the previous healee, and starting fresh. It reminds us to be fully in the present moment. It fulfills the same purpose in a mirror gazing ritual.

Some people choose to take a ritual shower or bath

prior to mirror gazing. A warm bath with candles and perhaps some aroma therapy helps to relax you and separates you from your everyday reality. Visualize all your cares being rinsed off and as you step out of the shower or tub imagine your cares being left behind in the water and being washed down the drain. Dry off with a soft towel, dress in your comfortable mirror gazing apparel and you are automatically in the right frame of mind to begin mirror gazing.

I would love to try mirror gazing while relaxing in a warm bath, but so far I have not had that opportunity. A friend of mine has a large bathtub with a seat so that you can sit upright in chest deep water (unlike regular bathtubs where you have your legs stretched out in front of you), and I think it would be interesting to mount a mirror on the wall in front of you in such a tub to see how it would work. Perhaps there would be problems with fog on the mirror from the hot water in the bath, but it certainly would be relaxing.

Could you mirror gaze in a hot tub? I haven't tried it, but I don't see why not if you had a comfortable place to sit and an appropriate spot to place your mirror.

Salt

Salt is a natural preservative and has been used in purification ceremonies for thousands of years. You can place a small bowl of sea salt near your mirror, or sprinkle a few grains around the area to create a sacred space. Wiccans often use salt to "cast a circle" or create a sacred space when performing sacred ceremonies. Afterwards the salt is swept up as part of the closing ritual.

We recently had a wonderful house blessing performed by Tibetan monks. In this ceremony the monks created a sacred space by chanting over dry rice and then sprinkling small amounts of the blessed rice around on the floor. We were told to then leave the rice on the floor until we felt compelled to sweep it up. In this case the rice represented abundance and prosperity.

Bowl of water

Many people find that water helps to magnetize or attract visions. It is also believed that it absorbs any negative energy in the room. You might want to pour a layer of sea salt into the bowl of water so that it forms a layer on the bottom of the bowl. At the end of the session, before pouring out the water, look carefully at the salt, sometimes you might find images formed in it.

Prayer

Prayer is a method of setting intention. The act of praying simply means putting into words exactly what you are hoping for, clarifying exactly what you want to have happen. By speaking the words out loud you are forcing yourself to clarify exactly what you want, which in this case is to have a vision. Have you ever noticed how when you think silently about something it is never quite as clear as when you say the words out loud? The spoken word is very powerful. When you pray out loud you are telling the universe what you want to have happen.

Who do you pray to? This depends on your belief system. In my own case, I pray to the universe, to the Infinite

Spirit that surrounds and connects all of us, but feel free to pray to whatever you consider your higher power to be.

If you are totally skeptical and do not believe in any sort of higher power it really doesn't matter, just state your intention, whether it is to find a solution to a problem, to talk to a dead loved one, or to have an out-of-body experience and wait to see what happens. Ask for protection if you think you need it.

My own prayer generally goes something like this:

Infinite Spirit, thank you for allowing me this opportunity to connect with the wisdom of the universe.

My intention for this session is to ..... (talk with my mother, get a solution to a business or personal problem, meet with my spirit guides, travel to ..., etc.)

I ask that everything that takes place, everything that I experience, will be for my highest and best. Thank you.

(**Note:** This last line is my version of asking for protection.)

Incense

Many people find incense very helpful in creating the right mood. The Catholic Church has used it very successfully for years. Personally I do not use incense because I am extremely sensitive to scents and it makes me dizzy and gives me a headache. Obviously, if it works for you then use it, if it doesn't work for you then don't use it.

Candles

Fire has traditionally been used to purify and cleanse a space. The easiest and safest way to benefit from the purifying effect of fire is to light a candle. I like to use candles in glass jars for safety, so that I am not distracted worrying that any wax will drip and I know that nothing will catch on fire while I am sitting in a semi-trance state staring into the mirror.

Soft music

I find soft music to be particularly useful in creating the right mood. I use a CD of music intended for Reiki sessions because it is very relaxing, and runs for a full hour without breaks between songs. Even if my mirror gazing session was to extend beyond one hour, (which it seldom has) by that time I would be so involved in the vision that the silence at the end of the CD would not bother me in the slightest.

Generally, I find that mirror gazing sessions end naturally sometime between a half an hour to an hour at which point I become totally conscious of my surroundings and I find myself conscious of being back sitting in my chair. Perhaps this is because I have unconsciously decided that this is long enough, or perhaps this is all that my butt can take of sitting in one position, I don't know which.

Ending the ritual and "closing" yourself off

Many people who are developing their psychic or mediumistic abilities find that they have difficulty "turning it off" but this is not a problem with mirror gazing, the ritual for ending a mirror gazing session is very simple. You just turn the mirror over (or cover it with a cloth if it is mounted on the wall), say a short prayer of thanks, and blow out the candles. Then put your tools away, hang up your ritual clothing (if you have any) and go about the rest of your day (since I tend to do this at night I simply put on my night gown and go to bed). You are now effectively "closed off."

More elaborate rituals

Throughout history the images and guidance that people got through scrying was considered a gift from the gods, a very serious business indeed and very elaborate rituals were devised to reflect the serious nature of the activity. Even today some people prefer more elaborate rituals. Lighting a particular number of candles in a particular order, walking around the room in a particular direction (clockwise or counter-clockwise), and invoking the guidance of particular angels are just a few of the things that some people choose to include in their rituals.

Fasting

I have heard it suggested that you should not eat anything for at least six hours before sitting down to scry, but I find it best to have some balance, you should have eaten something but not be overly full. Too hungry and you will be distracted by your empty stomach, while being too full makes it too easy to fall asleep.

Alcohol

Some people recommend that you do not drink any alcohol during the 24 hours prior to scrying, and yet other people scry quite successfully while drinking a glass of wine or a wee nip of whiskey. Once again I think the key is balance and moderation.

Personally I do not use alcohol simply because it does not make me feel good (I'm a cheap drunk, one small glass and my head starts to spin, two and I get sick, three and I'm under the table) but if you want to have a drink it probably won't be a problem, in fact it might help you to relax, while over indulging will definitely impede your ability to concentrate and would make the use of candles dangerous.

Sexual energy

I have heard people say that you should not engage in sexual relations on a day when you are planning to perform mirror gazing, and yet other people make use of sexual energy in rituals. Whatever, go ahead and make your own decision regarding this, I don't have an opinion on this one way or the other.

The "magic" is inside of you

Whether the ritual that you develop for your mirror gazing sessions is very simple or very elaborate, the important thing to remember is that the "magic" is actually inside you, not in the tools, the prayers, or the sequence of actions that you perform.

*"People only see
what they are prepared to see."*

Karl Popper

How to do it

While it is possible for mirror gazing visions to take place spontaneously most of us want to know how to deliberately call up the visions. So here are the steps that I have found to be most effective.

Collect your tools

You will need the following items:

- **a black scrying mirror** (or other scrying tool)

- **one or two candles**, preferably in glass containers for safety (you do not want to be distracted from your trance state worrying about fire safety)

- **matches or a lighter** to light the candles (being a non-smoker this is the one item I tend to forget)

- a small **bowl of water**

- a **table** upon which to place the mirror

- a comfortable **chair**

- some **meditation music**

Set up your space

The most important prerequisite for mirror gazing is that you have a quiet spot free of distractions. Ideally this is a separate room exclusively devoted to metaphysical work. However, most people don't have such an ideal place, so just find the most comfortable, quiet spot for you to set up.

Your scrying tools

All the items that you use for mirror gazing should be kept stored in a safe place where they will not be touched by other people. A drawer or a wooden box will work. Do not store anything else in this space that is not used in your mirror gazing.

Perform your ritual

As I explained in the previous chapter it is useful to perform some sort of ritual prior to beginning your mirror gazing session. What your ritual consists of is not so important. The main reason for performing the ritual is to signal to your mind your intention to connect with the universal unconscious, or the spirit world, whichever concept best resonates with you.

Silence

In our society it is very rare to experience total silence. Telephones are constantly ringing, televisions are on everywhere you go, and people continually listen to music from their iPods. Most people can't stand silence. Turn off your phone, turn off the television, and try to plan your scrying time when there will be no distractions. I can't imagine anything more upsetting than finally getting to visit with my mother and having the session cut off prematurely by some distraction.

Meditation music

Absolute silence is virtually impossible. If you live in a city you are continually being bombarded by street noise. Even if you are out somewhere totally isolated the sounds of nature can be deafening if you are trying to sit and meditate. So, in order to provide a sort of relaxing white noise in an otherwise distracting environment, it is a good idea to play some quiet meditation music.

Try to find a CD that does not have breaks since suddenly changing songs can be very jarring. Obviously you want something very subtle and unobtrusive. As much as I love drumming and chanting, this sort of music just doesn't work well for mirror gazing. If you are scrying in a home where other people are present you might want to try using earphones to listen to the music.

While it is ideal if your music runs on beyond the end of your session, if your session runs on longer than the length of your music CD and the music goes off you will probably find that you will be so involved with your vision that the sudden lack of music will not bother you. The most important thing is that your music lasts long enough for you to become involved in your vision.

Positioning your mirror

Place your mirror on a table, and place a comfortable chair in front of it. Ideally the chair should be one that allows you to lean back slightly and relax. Experiment with the positioning of the chair so that you are able to see the surface of the mirror but not see your own reflection. Then leave the mirror face down or covered with a cloth until you are ready to begin.

If you are using a crystal ball or a bowl of water you will want to position it on the table so that you can lean over it comfortably. Some people prefer to hold the crystal ball in their lap rather than placing it on the table.

Set out a bowl of water

If you are scrying with a bowl of water a second bowl of water is not necessary, but if you are using a mirror or a crystal ball you should set out a bowl of water somewhere on the table near you.

Water represents mystery and unseen forces. Many people find that the water helps to magnify or attract the visions. For much of history people believed that crystals were formed from solidified water. The word crystal comes from the Greek word "clear ice." When we scry we are accessing this ancient archetypal link between water and the unconscious mind.

Another reason for setting out the bowl of water is that many people believe that the water traps any negative energy, or residual energy from the session that might be circulating in the room. Immediately after the session you should empty the bowl of water down the drain.

Incense

Personally I am very sensitive to scents, and many other people are also, so I do not use incense either during my own meditation or during any of my classes, but many people find incense to be helpful in creating the special atmosphere associated with the mirror gazing trance state.

Light your candles

You should have a darkened room with candle light being the only source of light. With practice, some people manage to scry during the daylight, but at least initially you will probably find that it works best in a darkened room.

One of the main reasons why scrying is easier at night is because the dim lighting creates a form of visual sensory deprivation which is helpful to trance induction.

Light your candles just prior to beginning each session and put them out immediately afterward. Make sure that your candles are long enough that they will last beyond the end of your session so that your session won't be interrupted prematurely. It has traditionally been taught that the flame acts as a beacon for spirits who assist in the mirror gazing.

Scrying has traditionally been done at night because it was believed that the moon acts as a kind of gateway between our ordinary physical world and the mysterious realm of spirit. Also, it was believed that the unconscious mind is nearer the surface at night. Many people believe that scrying works best during the increasing phase of the moon (from the new moon to the full moon) and that it is less effective during the decreasing phase of the moon (from the full moon to the new moon). Test this theory out for yourself to see if you notice any effect.

Set up the candles to the side and behind you so that they do not distract your attention, or cause a reflection on the surface of the speculum. The flickering of the candles or electric candle lamps placed outside of your range of vision, along with the lack of a horizon line and absence of color on the speculum combine to produce a trance state and induce "hallucinations." This is a scientifically proven effect is called the Ganzfeld effect. I put the word "hallucinations" in quotation marks because once you experience it you will not be inclined to believe that you are hallucinating.

WARNING: The flickering of candles has been known to cause epileptic seizures in susceptible individuals. However, since by the time we reach adulthood in our society we have all been exposed to candle light either at Christmas time or at expensive restaurant dinners, by now you should know if you can tolerate the flickering of candle light. Obviously, if you know that you have a problem with seizures caused by flickering candle light then do not use them.

Relaxed expectation

Start with a sense of relaxed expectation. In other words, you are looking forward to the experience, you know something is going to happen, but you are not trying to force it. Relax. If you are using a mirror lean back, but if you are using a bowl of water or a crystal ball lean over it, looking in.

Initially concentrate on the dark surface of the speculum,

and consciously feel your body relaxing. But then allow your eyes to look beyond the surface as if into the center of the darkness. Let your eyes become unfocused, more like gazing off into the distance at nothing. Relax and let your mind drift, allow it to slip into the state between awake and asleep.

The self hypnotic state

What you are doing is allowing yourself to fall into an altered state. You are, in effect, hypnotizing yourself. We do this all the time. In this state your conscious mind takes a break and lets what is on your unconscious mind pop to the surface.

When a vision begins to form it usually appears like clouds in the sky. At first it might appear to be taking place on the surface of the speculum but then sometimes it is like the image is in your mind and the speculum will disappear completely and it will seem like you are in the image.

Be patient with yourself. Sometimes nothing will happen, you just aren't clicking. Other times the results will astound you. Generally it gets easier each time you do it. Over time the visions will come faster and clearer.

The Ganzfeld Effect, or "prisoner's cinema." There are numerous accounts of people in low light situations experiencing spontaneous visions. Miners trapped underground and prisoners in solitary confinement have told of seeing angels, Jesus, the Virgin Mary, or deceased loved ones who came to help and keep them company during difficult times. With mirror gazing we are attempting to experience the same thing without the accompanying trauma.

How often should you scry?

Initially you could try to set aside some time each night for this work. The more often you practice the better you will get. However, as with everything in life, it is possible to overdo it.

Connecting with the spirit world is very exciting, and making contact with departed loved ones is the most wonderful thing imaginable when it happens, but we are still alive, we still have our own lives to live. I like to use mirror gazing for help with my business and for creative suggestions for my art, but we cannot let ourselves become too dependent on it.

Go ahead and do it daily, it is a great form of meditation, but if you find yourself spending too much time interacting with the spirit world and not enough time interacting with living people it is definitely time to cut back. Moderation is the key.

Give the universe some advance notice if at all possible

Try announcing your intention earlier in the day, or even a few days earlier if you know when you are going to be sitting down to mirror gaze. Say it out loud. Give the universe, and your loved ones in spirit a heads up so that they can make plans to visit you. It is like saying "I'll be home on Friday evening why don't you come over." Don't just expect that they will be available that day without any warning.

Set your intention in advance, decide what you are hoping to achieve during the session, but do not be too insistent on the outcome. The universe always gives us what we need, but not always what we want or expect.

If your intention is to come up with a solution to a business problem, or a creative block, tell the universe what you are looking for. Give your unconscious mind some advance warning to work out a solution.

Consider what you eat prior to your session

Although some people choose to fast prior to mirror gazing, I think it is best to have eaten something before I sit. It is too hard to relax into a trance state if you are hungry. But also try not to overeat prior to a mirror gazing session. Too much food will put you to sleep.

I remember hearing old mediums say how that they would eat sweets prior to performing mediumship, and I thought this was just an excuse, until I noticed that when I went on a very low carb diet my ability to connect with the other side was seriously impaired. So, it might be an idea to experiment with having some candy prior to your session to see how it affects you.

Many people say that you should not consume any caffeine prior to mirror gazing, but I have not found that it affects me in the slightest; in fact, I find that a nice cup of tea before I start is exactly what I need. I remember taking a mediumship class with Janet Nohavec (one of the best mediums that I have ever witnessed) and hearing her jokingly say that she needed to have just the perfect amount of Starbucks coffee in order to do her best work. Obviously if caffeine impedes your ability to connect then don't drink it, but otherwise feel free to indulge.

While I am on the topic of indulging, some of the best mediums and psychics in history had a tendency to overindulge in alcohol, so while I am not encouraging this, I think it shows that being overly careful about what we eat or drink is not absolutely necessary in order to make contact with the spirit world.

Scrying with a partner

Most of the time mirror gazing is a solitary activity. I encourage it for personal psychic development and developing your creativity. But it is possible to scry with a partner.

One reason why you might want to do it with another person is so the other person can record the information you are getting when you get it. If you have a tendency to forget some of what you saw or heard after you finish then this would be convenient. In this case you would have some sort of recording device handy and you would dictate everything as it takes place. Your partner could handle starting and stopping the recorder so that your trance state is not interrupted. They could also take notes for you. In this case you would not want to be sitting too close to the other person otherwise the energy, and the messages, could get confused. You should be sitting as far apart as is practical, at least an arm length apart.

I did not realize how important this was until I was teaching a mirror gazing class where the students were seated too close together. After the session when everyone was talking about what they had experienced one woman said that she had seen a long series of animals walking in one side and going out the other side of her mirror. There were farm animals, house pets, birds, all sorts of animals. She had no idea what this was about, she couldn't understand what the message was for her, she did not know what the significance could possibly be. I had no idea why she had seen this until I noticed who she was sitting next to. It turns out that the woman seated very close beside her was a veterinarian, and the animals had been walking in the veterinarian's direction. Interestingly, the veterinarian did not see the animals, instead she got some other jumbled visions that did not seem to apply to her. Both students still found it fascinating that they were able to see something so vividly in the mirror on their first attempt, but I have made it a point to make sure that the students were not seated so closely after that.

Something else this experience proved to me was that there is more to mirror gazing than simply tapping into our own unconscious memories.

Another reason why you might want to do it with another person is so that you can get information for them. Personally I think that everyone should learn how to do this for themselves and make the contact directly, but I can see where there might be cases where someone has gone through a particularly difficult time and wants some advice immediately so they could turn to a friend who was adept at mirror gazing to see if they could get something for them.

Basically, if you are scrying for someone else you would want to be sitting close together so that you could be in the other person's energy and pick up their messages.

Keep a scrying journal

Get yourself a book and record the details of each session immediately after the session while it is still fresh in your mind. Make sure and include everything that takes place because you will often find that small details that seem to be of no significance at the time will turn out to be the most important. Especially where future events are concerned, it is very common for people to see a symbol and not understand what it means and then after the event takes place the meaning becomes apparent. This does not mean that predictions are worthless. It just means that sometimes it takes time and practice for us to understand what the various symbols mean for us.

Write down the time, place, and date of the session. Make note of the phase of the moon to see if that has an effect on your experience. Make note of what you ate or drank, what your emotional state was, how you felt physically, what the weather was like (some people find that rainy days work best) etc. Over time you will probably start to see a pattern, it will become apparent that certain conditions work better for you. Leave space in your book so that you can go back later and add additional comments.

That is pretty much all there is to it

So, that is it. As you can see, there is nothing particularly difficult or mysterious about mirror gazing. It does not require expensive tools and it is something that anyone who has an interest is capable of doing. The following chapter contains some exercises that can help you do it a little better.

Exercises to improve your ability   8

Do you have to be a particularly gifted psychic in order to mirror gaze?

No, I don't think so. This is something that anyone who has the desire and a willingness to practice can do.

Not all authors agree with me though. In the book *"Hygienic Clairvoyance"* by Jacob Dixon (an abridgement of which is reprinted in Appendix C) the author claims that the general population is divided into six progressively more profound levels of ability.

Dixon claims that 63% of people can become what he calls "sensitives." In other words, he states that 63% of the population can develop some degree of psychic ability while the remaining 37% of people have no psychic ability at all. Dixon goes on to claim that 45% of the population can reach what he refers to as the second stage of clairvoyance, which means that they have slightly more psychic ability. 32% can reach the third stage, 14% can reach the fourth stage, 5% can reach the fifth stage, and only 2% can reach the highest or sixth stage.

I think that these percentages are completely off. In my experience, everyone has some degree of instinctive, natural psychic ability that can be developed further.

Everyone gets "hunches" or "gut feelings"

I have found that everyone has experienced some sort of psychic experience at some point in their life. This psychic experience can be as simple as getting an uneasy feeling about a particular person or situation for no apparent reason. Everyone gets "hunches," or "gut feelings," whether we choose to act on them or not. The more often that you pay attention to these feelings or "hunches" and act on them, the more often you will experience them. It is simply a matter of choosing to pay attention.

Many times people don't admit that they depend on their intuition because they think it would sound absurd, and open them up to ridicule, but everyone uses it to some degree. Even people in supposedly logical or analytical careers, like accountants, depend on their intuition (even if they don't realize that they are doing so), and they find that it gets more accurate the longer they are on the job.

I remember having a conversation with a forensic accountant (someone who analyses financial information looking for fraud) who told me that he uses his intuition all the time, he called it "the sniff test." He explained that most crooks at least make an attempt to cover their tracks, so at first glance the financial statements look perfectly fine, but that he gets a feeling, or a sense that something "smells bad" and when he gets this feeling he knows that he has to look more closely. He told me that often he awakens in the middle of the night "knowing" exactly where to look to find the evidence.

Auditors (accountants who verify and attest to the validity of company financial statements) use their intuition all the time. It is impossible for them to look at every transaction a company makes, so they look at sample transactions to check for problems, and often they use their intuition to guide them in asking the right questions of the right individuals.

"Whether you think you can, or you think you can't, you are right."

This quote has been attributed to Henry Ford. He understood one of the most important laws of life. If you think you can't do something (in this case you can't develop your psychic abilities) you won't put out the necessary effort to do so and will thereby "prove" that you can't do it. However, if you think you can do something, even if you do not succeed initially, you will put in the necessary effort and will eventually succeed.

Another way of saying this is that you always get what you expect. I see this all the time in mediumship development classes. People claim that they don't "get" anything (they don't see or hear spirit messages). A spirit could be doing a tap dance in front of them and they wouldn't notice. It really isn't that they don't "see" it, rather they don't expect to see it and so their rational mind censors what they are experiencing.

In the past, young children were often used for scrying because they had not yet developed this rational censoring mind, they didn't yet "know" that it was "impossible" and would simply say what they saw.

Since you will only "get" what you expect to get, if you believe that you are one of Dixon's 37% who have no psychic ability then it is true that you will never experience any psychic phenomena.

A psychic aristocracy?

I get so annoyed when I hear some celebrity psychic or medium claiming that they have some special gift. They make out that it just fell into their lap with no effort on their part. They forget to mention how hard they worked to develop their "gift." Often they imply that it is more of a curse than a blessing.

I particularly hate it when I hear that it is an inherited gift. The notion that only certain people have this ability is elitist, and self-serving. Obviously, if only certain people have the "gift" then if you want a message you have to go to those people, and this is where the potential for fraud and manipulation comes in. But if you realize that everyone can do this, that everyone can develop their own direct connection, then you are no longer at the mercy of charlatans.

Mirror gazing is one technique that can help you to discover the natural inherent psychic abilities that you already possess.

Male vs. female?

Currently, more women perform mirror gazing than

men, and some people claim that it is easier for women than for men, but I suspect that this is more a matter of desire than innate ability.

The most famous scryers throughout history such as Nostradamus, Kenneth MacKenzie, and Dr. John Dee were men, and yet the priestesses at Delphi were women, so I don't think that the sex of the individual makes any difference. However, I have noticed in my classes that some men are more self confident, and are therefore more willing to talk in front of the class about what they witnessed in the mirror. I think this self confidence is part of what makes it appear that some people are better at it than others.

Could you be the Wayne Gretzky of mirror gazing?

Okay, so I'm a Canadian and we use hockey analogies. I realize that while anyone can learn to play hockey to some degree (even physically handicapped people as proven by the amazing athletes at the Para Olympics) not everyone can play like Wayne Gretzky. So maybe you won't be the Wayne Gretzky of mirror gazing, but you can certainly learn to play well enough to achieve your own personal goals.

I remember watching an interview with Wayne Gretzky and the interviewer asked him how parents could motivate their kids to practice. His reply stuck in my mind. He said that no one ever had to persuade him to practice; in fact, his parents had to drag him off the ice at bed time. He was self motivated. He played because he loved to play. Yes, he obviously started off with something of a gift, an innate talent, but he became "the Great One" because he enjoyed what he was doing and because he enjoyed it he practiced all the time.

So, like everything else, if you want to be successful at mirror gazing you have to work at it. Every time you sit down to scry you create a conditioned response, and each time you do this it becomes easier for you to enter into the self hypnotic state necessary for seeing visions. Practice is essential, but it should be enjoyable. In mirror gazing, as in anything else in life, if it isn't fun you won't put enough effort into it to be really successful.

Training your mind to develop your psychic ability is very similar to training your body to perform a particular sport. It's a matter of practice.

What if you can't visualize?

Many people claim that they cannot visualize objects or events. I used to think this too. I knew that I could feel, hear, sense, and even smell things, but when I closed my eyes all I saw was black. My brother described being able to see things play out like a movie screen in front of his eyes, and I really wished that it was like that for me.

Many years ago I was taking a development class with John White in Lily Dale, New York and he was talking about visualizing. (Note: John is a great teacher, and if you ever have the opportunity I highly recommend his classes.) I put up my hand and said that I couldn't visualize the way other people do, that for me it was more sensing than visualizing. I have never forgotten his response.

He replied, *"Never assume that you see things any differently than anyone else. You can never really know what the experience is for someone else; words cannot accurately describe what we are experiencing. We call it "seeing" but clairvoyance is only part of it."*

My initial reaction to his answer was annoyance (well actually, annoyance doesn't really describe what I was feeling; I was embarrassed and angry!) I felt that he didn't understand that I was "different," that it was harder for me than it was for everyone else. How dare he!

To illustrate what he meant he told us all to close our eyes and just sit still. He asked us to think about our kitchen at home. He told us to think about the refrigerator, the stove, the sink. Then think about going over to the fridge and opening the door.

"Take a lemon out of the fridge, wash it under running water and place it on a cutting board. Get out a sharp knife and cut the lemon into quarters. As you cut into it the lemon squirts out some juice. You pick up one of the pieces and bite into it...."

At that point the room erupted into squeals, we had all experienced the mouth puckering sensation of biting into a lemon.

At that moment I finally understood what it was to "see" something. John was right, unless you have a brain injury that affects your memory, if you can remember what your kitchen looks like (it doesn't have to be in great detail, but enough to remember where the fridge is) then you are capable of "visualizing."

Training the mind

It has often been said that the mind is like a spoiled two-year-old when his mother is on the phone, constantly wanting attention. The minute you sit down to meditate or to scry, a million other thoughts jump into your attention. Suddenly you find yourself thinking about what to make for dinner, an incident that took place in the third grade, or you get a sudden urge to get up and pay the phone bill. If you do manage to calm your mind for a moment then your body gets involved, suddenly you develop an irritating itch, your butt goes numb, or you find yourself yawning.

As any mother of a two-year-old soon discovers, it is futile to attempt to force matters. Distraction is the answer. These following exercises are the equivalent of giving a child a cookie or a coloring book and crayons.

Monkey mind

In Buddhism the tendency of our mind to jump around frantically from one thought to another is sometimes referred to as "monkey mind." You control monkey mind by giving your conscious mind something to focus on.

In parts of India and Thailand hunters use a similar idea to trap monkeys. On one side of a coconut they make a hole just large enough for a monkey to insert its hand; then on the other side they drill a small hole through which they thread a long knotted rope. They place some sort of treat inside the hollowed out coconut and sit just out of sight waiting for a monkey to go for the treat. The monkey reaches inside to grab the treat but with his hand clenched around the treat he cannot remove it from the coconut. The hunter then reels in the monkey like a fisherman reeling in a fish. The monkey gets caught because it won't let go of the treat.

Exercises that you can do to control your mind and improve your ability to "see"

It is not absolutely necessary to do any of these exercises in order to mirror gaze successfully. Many people experience incredible things the first time they look into the mirror, but if you want to improve your visualization skills, or simply learn how to relax, you can do these exercises at random times throughout the day when you have a few minutes free. They are particularly effective in increasing your ability to stay focused on one particular thought and thereby control monkey mind. If you just have fun and don't struggle with these exercises you will find them very relaxing. Regardless of how badly you think you are doing at first, as time goes on you will be amazed at your progress.

Simple objects

This is a very easy exercise that you can do anytime that you have a minute or two when you can close your eyes. There are no other props or tools required for this one.

Simply sit down, relax, and look at some object near you. It doesn't matter what the object is. For example, right now as I sit here at my computer desk there are numerous items that I can choose from, a pen, the desk lamp, my water bottle, the phone, it doesn't matter, just get it firmly in your mind and then close your eyes. With your eyes closed "visualize" the object. If you find that you can't "see" it just open your eyes and take another look at it.

Once you can do that easily you can progress to altering the appearance of the object. Make it bigger or smaller. Distort it and then bring it back to its original shape. Change the color. Just play with it.

Morphing shapes

This exercise is a progression from the simple objects exercise. In this case you do not have an item in front of you to look at, it exists only in your mind. It is a bit like a screen saver I used to have on my computer.

Simply close your eyes, relax, and "see" a square. Make the square larger, and then smaller, distort it, turn it into a diamond shape then back into a square. Make it three dimensional by turning it into a cube. Stretch it out and turn it into a rectangle.

Experiment with colors, make it red, orange, yellow, green, blue, purple. Make each side a different color, and then blur the colors into each other.

Spin the shape around slowly, then faster, and then slow it down again.

Soften the edges, morph the shape into a circle, then make it three dimensional and turn it into a ball, make the ball spin, then bounce, color it in solid colors, then patterns.

Experiment with different shapes, morph one into the next, first a square, then a triangle, then add sides, first 5 sides, then 6 sides, then 7 sides, then 8. Smooth the 8 sides into a circle, and then turn it into an oval, and back into a square. See how smooth and seamless the transitions can become.

This is a great game to play when you are at the dentist, or during other minor medical procedures. When you are able to focus completely on the morphing shapes you will be amazed to find that you don't notice any discomfort.

Rose bud

Once you are adept at visualizing simple objects and morphing shapes you can try this rose bud exercise. This is the first exercise that involves the sense of smell and touch. Sit still, you don't actually touch a rose with your hands, all of the action takes place in your mind.

Close your eyes and imagine a tightly closed rose bud. "See" the stem, the thorns, and the leaves. "See" the color of the petals, notice how the green of the stem is lighter in some places and darker in others, blending to almost yellow at the point of the thorns.

Watch as the rose bud begins to slowly loosen, then each petal begins to open up. Notice the way the color of the petals seems darker toward the center, and lighter toward the tips.

When the rose is fully open, "smell" the beautiful fragrance, and "feel" the velvety softness of the petals against your cheek.

Experiment with opening up the rose bud then closing

it back up again a few times, then open the rose up fully and watch it begin to droop, watch the petals turn darker and the edges curl, and then one by one they fall off leaving just the rose hip in the center.

If you get really good at this you can try reversing the process. Re-create the rose, starting with just the rose hip and watch the petals go back into place, watch the curled edges straighten out, see the color come back. Then watch the petals as they tighten back into a rose bud.

Morphing numbers

This one is similar to the morphing shapes exercise. If you are an analytical type person who likes to measure your progress you will like this one. For this exercise you will need a minute timer, a piece of paper and a pen or pencil.

Set the timer for either 1 or 2 minutes. It is amazing how long 2 minutes can seem when you first begin.

Close your eyes and "see" the number 1. Write it out in your mind as though you were writing it on a piece of paper, then watch it morph into a three dimensional shape. Then do the same thing with the number 2, then 3, and on and on.

Every time that you get distracted and fail to keep the number clearly in your mind you have to start again at number one. When the timer goes off write down the number you got to. As time goes on you can increase the timer to 5 minutes, then 10 minutes.

Your progress in this will seem sporadic. Some days

you will do better than others. Don't stress yourself over your apparent lack of progress. Over time you will improve.

If you don't have a minute timer, a variation on this exercise is to record the time when you begin and then keep going until you reach a particular number, perhaps 30 to begin with. Same as previously, every time you get distracted and lose the number you start again from 1. When you finally reach your goal number open your eyes and record the time. Gradually you will find that you can reach your goal number faster and faster.

If, at first, you find that variation too difficult you can simply record the time that you start and then go as far as you can before you get distracted. Then simply open your eyes and record the time and the number that you reached.

I like the challenge aspect of this number exercise, but if you find yourself getting stressed about wanting to "succeed" and feel bad about your apparent lack of progress, then forget it and use the other exercises instead.

Spirit body exercise

This spirit body exercise is to remind us that we are much more than a physical body.

Sit comfortably and close your eyes. Without moving, visualize raising your right hand and hold it up in front of your face, "see" it clearly, turn your hand over and "see" the palm. Clench your fingers, reach out and grab something,

This is your spirit body. Even though you are sitting

still, your mind has the sensation that you are actually moving. Athletes can use this to practice performing sports, and musicians can practice a piece of music in this manner.

I remember reading an account of a US soldier who spent several years as a prisoner during the Vietnam war. Prior to the war he enjoyed the game of golf but was a mediocre player. While in captivity he spent hours every day imagining that he was playing golf. When he was released and returned home he was amazed to discover that in spite of it being years since he had been out on a course his golf game had actually improved dramatically, he was able to play at the level he had been visualizing. Also, he had not lost nearly as much muscle condition as his fellow prisoners because in spite of being sedentary his body "thought" he was regularly exercising.

Your secret place

The following is an exercise that I have been told was originally developed by the US military to prepare soldiers to cope in the event that they are captured and tortured. It is intended to help maintain their sanity in spite of difficult situations. I was told about it by a student in my mirror gazing class who had been taught it while in the services. Most of us will never need to use it in the type of horrific situations that they are being trained for, but it is excellent for developing your confidence in moving around in your spirit body.

The point of this exercise is to create a mental space where you can go to relax, to escape from traumatic situations in the "real" world, or to meet with deceased loved ones, and spirit guides or mentors.

Basically, you are going to create an imaginary world, and become as familiar with it as you are with the real world around you. You are creating your own pocket universe - no one else knows that it exists - spirit visitors only come by invitation. This is a totally safe place, no living people can come into this world

This world can be whatever you want, you are not limited by any of our physical laws, it can be your own science fiction world, make it whatever feels good for you, choose colors that appeal to you.

Close your eyes and relax. Start by mentally looking around and envisioning the area immediately around you. The idea is to create a place that you will come back to consistently, so create something that is appealing to you. Get very detailed. Start with a beautiful intimate spot with comfortable seating where you can meet with your spirit visitors. Look carefully at all the details. Get to know the area intimately.

Affirm your secret place's invulnerability -- you are totally safe in this place. Anyone that you meet in this place is your friend. No one can stay if you ask them to leave. This is your private world.

Exploring your private world

Once you are totally familiar with your immediate surroundings you can choose to begin exploring farther afield. Make you universe larger and larger while keeping in mind that you are not constrained by time or distance. Travel in your world is instantaneous.

Come back to this place regularly in your meditation time. The more often you come, the more vivid and real it will become to you.

Practice using all of your senses. See the things around you, notice as the faces of your spirit friends come into view, listen to the sounds of nature and to the voices of your spirit friends. Utilize your sense of smell. Taste ripe luscious fruit, and drink cold clean water. Feel the sun on your skin and the wind blowing in your hair.

Each time you go back to your private world you will find it easier and easier until this world feels as real to you as the physical world you live in.

Memories of past events

Here is one final exercise that can do far more for you than just improve your mirror gazing skills. This one can change your life completely. In this exercise you practice re-living past events.

Sit down, close your eyes, relax, and remember a particularly happy memory. Relive it exactly as it happened to you. This is a relatively easy thing for most people, and it is very useful for improving your mood in a hurry.

For a little more of a challenge, sit down, close your eyes and visualize an unpleasant memory from your past. Once you can see and feel the event clearly it is time to start modifying the memory. Try running through the memory again from the beginning but change it to make it less unpleasant, change the action, and change the dialogue. Keep improving it until you make it the way you wish it had been. Notice how differently you feel. Replay it over and over the new way until you succeed in forgetting the original and only remember the modified version.

This exercise shows us that we can choose to feel good or bad depending on how we think about the events in our lives. The actual event is not as important as the way we think about the event. This exercise clearly illustrates how our feelings are influenced by our thoughts.

So, if you want to change how you feel first change your thoughts.

Some people are naturals, while others have to develop their psychic skills

As I pointed out at the beginning of this chapter, I am convinced that anyone can perform mirror gazing. Sure, some people are "naturals" who can do it the first time they look into a mirror while others need some time and practice to develop their skills. But don't feel bad if it doesn't come to you immediately.

As with many other skills that people struggle to develop, I have noticed that the people who have to work to develop their skills ultimately become more adept than those who come by it easily. People who "get it" immediately usually don't work to improve their skills and stay at their initial skill level, while people who have the discipline to work and practice ultimately advance far beyond that of someone who is a "natural."

Have fun!

Mirror gazing is supposed to be fun and relaxing, just like these exercises are supposed to be fun and relaxing. So don't take it too seriously, remember to have fun.

Appendix A - How to Read the Crystal

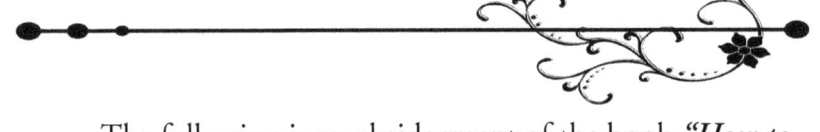

The following is an abridgement of the book *"How to Read the Crystal"* by Sepharial. This short book was originally published by London Foulsham & Co. Ltd. in London, England in 1922. It has been edited slightly for ease in reading.

Who was Sepharial?

Sepharial was the pen name of the English Theosophist Dr. Walter Gorn Old (1864-1929). Although he originally studied medicine, he became a well-known astrologer and student of metaphysics who wrote numerous books on occult topics. He was one of the "Inner Circle" of 12 disciples of Madam Helena Blavatsky and was one of the founding members of the Theosophical movement in England. He lived with Madame Blavatsky during her years in England up until her death. She called him *"The Astral Tramp"* because of his nightly visits to the astral plane.

The Crystal

The crystal itself is a clear piece of quartz or beryl, sometimes oval in shape, but more generally spheroid. It is accredited by Reichenbach and other researchers with highly magnetic qualities capable of producing in a suitable subject a state analogous to the ordinary waking trance of the hypnotist.

It is believed that all bodies convey, or are the vehicles of, a certain universal magnetic property, variously called Od, Odyle, etc., which is regarded as an inert and passive substance underlying the more active forces familiar to us in kinetic, calorific, and electrical phenomena. In this respect it bears a position analogous to the Argon of the atmosphere. It is capable of taking up, sympathetically, the vibrations of those bodies or elements to which it is temporarily related. But of itself it has no activity, although in its still, and calm depths it holds the potentiality of all magnetic forces. This Odyle, then, is particularly potent in the quartz or beryl, when brought into activity by the intention of the seer. It produces and retains more readily in that form the various images communicated to it from the soul of man. And the soul, in this connection, must be regarded as the repository of all that complex mass of emotions, thoughts, impressions, perceptions, feelings, etc., included in the inner life of man; for the soul of man is not the less a scientific fact because there are those who bandy words concerning its origin and nature.

It should not be a matter of surprise to learn that the crystal exerts a very definite and sensible effect upon the nervous system of a certain order of subjects. It does not affect all alike, nor act in exactly the same way on those whom

> **Editor's Note:** The author is expressing the 19th century belief that the crystal exerted a sort of magnetic effect on the brain of the scryer. We now know that these visions are a natural function of the brain and do not require any external magnetizing influence.

it does so affect. Where its action is more or less rapid and remarkable, the quartz or beryl crystal may be taken as the most effective medium for producing the vision. In other cases the concave mirror, either of polished copper or black japan, will be found serviceable for inducing the clairvoyant state.

In some other cases, again, a bowl of water is sufficient. The ecstatic vision was first induced in the case of Jacob Boehme by the sun's rays falling upon a bowl of water which caught and dazzled his eyes while he was engaged in the humble task of cobbling a pair of shoes. As a consequence of this exaltation of the sense of sight we have those remarkable works, *"The Aurora," "The Four Complexions," "The Signatura Rerum,"* and many others, together with a volume of letters and commentaries which, in addition to being of a highly spiritual nature, must also be regarded as scholarly when referred to their authorship.

In cases like the above it may be said that the clairvoyant faculty is constitutional and already fully developed, waiting only the circumstances which shall serve to bring it into active play, Emanuel Swedenborg, if we remember rightly, was 54 years of age before he awoke to the consciousness of his spiritual vision.

The medium employed for inducing the clairvoyant state cannot be definitely prescribed. It must remain a matter of experiment for each investigator. This, however, may be said: Every person whose life is not wholly sunk in selfish and material pleasures, but in whom the aspiration to a nobler and purer life is a hunger the world cannot satisfy, has within him the power to see and know that which he seeks behind the veil of his earthly senses. Nature has never produced a desire she could not satisfy. There is no hope, however vague, that the soul cannot define, and no aspiration, however high, that the wings of the spirit cannot reach. Therefore be patient and strive.

That there are some in whom the psychic faculties are more prone to activity than in others is certain, as also some in whom these powers are native. In others, the determination of the natural powers takes a more practical and mundane tendency, making them more successful in the affairs of daily life than in aught of a spiritual nature St. Paul has spoken of a diversity of gifts. "One star differeth from another in glory," he says, in very truth. This distribution of natural gifts proceeds from the celestial world, and is so ordered that each person born on this earth may fulfill his part in the economy of life. And because the spiritual needs of mankind are of primary importance, there are those born in whom the power of spiritual interpretation is the dominant faculty, such persons being the natural channels of intercourse between the superior and inferior worlds. These are to mankind what a certain order of microbial life is to the body of man-organic interpreters, translating the elements of food into blood, nerve, fiber, tissue, etc., agreeably to the laws of their being.

For those who would aspire to the gift of pure vision,

and in whom the faculty is striving for expression, the following pages are written. To others we would say, be content. All birds are not eagles. The nightingale has a song, the humming-bird a plumage which the eagle will never possess. The nightingale may sing to the stars, humming-bird to the flowers, but the eagle, whose tireless eyes gaze into the heart of day, is uncompanioned in its lofty loneliness in the barren mountain-tops.

Warning

There are in existence certain magical works, such as those of Trithemius and Barrett, wherein the use of the crystal is accompanied by certain rites and invocations. This ceremonial magic we are disposed to repudiate as highly dangerous. It brings into play a number of forces which may well prove disastrous in inexperienced hands. All action and reaction are equal and opposite. A child might easily fire a cannon, but could not possibly withstand its recoil. So in the education of the spiritual faculties, it is better to encourage their natural development by legitimate exercise than to invoke the action of stimulants which we may not afterwards be able to control. The continual fretting of the water will wear away a rock, though none doubts the water is softer than the rock. If the barrier between this and the soul-world be like granite, yet the patient and persistent action of a determined mind will sooner or later wear it away, the last layer will break down, and the light will stream through, dazzling the unaccustomed eyes with its effulgence.

It is our desire to indicate by what means and by what persons the natural development of the clairvoyant faculty may be achieved.

First, in regard to the subject, medium or seer. There are two distinct temperaments in which the faculty is likely to be dominant. There is the nervous temperament associated with a high muscular development, classified as the "mental-motive" temperament. It is characterized by extreme activity of body and mind and a certain nervous excitability. This type represents the positive seers, in whom the mind goes out towards the images of the soul. The other, in whom the passive temperament is predominate are those to whom the soul-images come by passive reflection, as things mirrored in a calm lake.

These two types - of which there are many varieties - achieve their psychic development by quite opposite means. The positive seer works with effort, throwing out the soul-images by the power of his will, perceiving them with more or less accuracy, and thereafter turning them over in the mind, reasoning and questioning concerning their import and meaning. The passive seer, on the contrary, works not at all and makes no effort, the visions coming slowly, almost imperceptibly, and in most cases having a literal interpretation. The visions in this case are not allegorical, emblematic, or symbolic, as in the case of the positive seer, but are actual visions of facts just as they have happened, or will transpire in the future. Of the two orders, the passive is the more serviceable because the more perspicuous, but it has the disadvantage of being largely under the control of external influences, and hence is frequently incapable of "seeing" anything whatever.

The positive type of seer exercises an introspective vision, searching inwardly towards the soul-world whence the revelations proceed. Of what nature these revelations are will appear in the following pages. The passive type of seer, on the contrary, remains in status quo, open to impressions coming inwards towards the perceptive faculty, but making no effort towards either outward or inward searching. The success of each depends upon the observance of that method which is agreeable to their respective temperaments.

In regard to the qualifications which should supplement and sustain the natural aptitude of the seer, the following remarks may be of general service.

Self-possession and confidence in one's own soul-faculties must be the firm rock upon which all revelations should rest. The purer the intention and motive of the seer, the more lucid will be the visions accorded. No reliable vision can be obtained by one whose nature is not inherently truthful. Any selfish desire dominating the mind in regard to any thing or person will distort the visions and render them misleading, while a persistent self-seeking spirit will effectually shut the doors upon all visions whatsoever. Therefore, above all things it is essential for the investigator to have an unflinching love of truth, to be resigned to the will of Heaven, to accept the revelations accorded in a spirit of grateful confidence, and finally to dispel all doubt and controversy by appeal to the eyes of one's own immortal soul. These are qualifications with which the seer should be invested, and if with these the quest is unsuccessful after a period of earnest trial, it must be taken as sufficient warrant that the faculty is not in the category of one's individual powers. Happily, the same qualifications brought to bear upon some other psychic faculty will result in a rich recompense.

Preliminaries

Having obtained a good crystal, as free as possible from blemish, care must be taken to keep it is much as possible in a dark place when not in use. The best covering therefore is a black one of soft material, such as velvet, which will not scratch the polished surface of the quartz.

Exposure to the sun's rays not only scores the face of the crystal, but also puts the odylic substance into activity, distributing and dissipating the magnetic force stored up therein.

It must not be understood that the visions are in the crystal itself. They are in the soul of the seer. But the odylic substance is acted upon by the nervo-vital emanations of the body of the seer, and reacts upon the brain centers by means of the optic nerves. That is why it is necessary to keep the crystal as free as possible from disturbing elements. For the same reason, when in use, the crystal should be overshadowed by the seer, and so placed that no direct rays of light from sun, or lamp may fall upon it. The odyle, as has been already stated, rapidly responds to surrounding magnetic conditions, and to the vibrations of surrounding bodies, and to none more powerfully than the etheric perturbation caused by combustion-indeed, to light of any kind.

For similar reasons the room in which the sitting is conducted should be only moderately warm and as shady as possible, provided it be not actually dark. A light by which one can just see to read average print is sufficient for the purpose in view.

> **Editor's Note**: Most modern scryers agree that dim light is more conducive to achieving the appropriate mental state for experiencing visions.

The crystal with which we have had the most satisfactory and surprising results is a cube of fine azure beryl, the deep blue of its serene depths being peculiarly restful and inspiring. But, as we have said, nothing is more effective than the white quartz crystal when found suitable.

It is important that all persons sitting in the same room as the seer be at arm's length away from him-farther if possible. Silence should be uniformly observed by those present. A recorder should be at hand to set down everything the seer may give voice to. If any questions are addressed to the seer while the sitting is in progress, they should be spoken in an undertone and as nearly a monotone as may be so that the seer is not suddenly surprised into consciousness of his surroundings, and the psychic thread thereby broken.

At first the sittings should not be of longer duration than fifteen minutes, but it is important they should take place regularly, every day if possible, and always at the same hour and in the same place. By this method of procedure it will be found that a cumulative effect is produced and success more speedily ensured. The reason is obvious, all actions tend to repeat themselves, to become automatic, to pass from the purposive into the habitual, and hence the psychic faculties will, if actuated at any set time and place, tend to bestir themselves towards the same end as that to which they were first moved by the conscious will and intention of the seer.

Until definite and satisfactory results are obtained, not more than two persons should be present at the sittings, and these should be in sympathy with the seer and each other. When the sitting is over, it will be found agreeable and useful to discuss the results obtained; or if none are elicited, the seer can give an account of his or her impressions and feelings during the sitting. It will be interesting to note these experiences and to compare them from time to time.

The seer or seers must not be disheartened if at the first few sittings nothing momentous takes place, but must persevere, with patience and self-control. Indeed, when one comes to consider the fact that for hundreds of generations the psychic faculties inherent in mankind have lain in absolute neglect, that perhaps the faculty of "clear vision" has never yet been brought into activity by any save the most remote of our ancestors, it will not be thought remarkable that it should be at first difficult to get any definite results. Rather should it be a matter of surprise that the power is still with us, that it is not wholly irresponsive to the voice of the soul.

While, in the course of physical evolution, many important functions have undergone remarkable changes, and organs, once active and useful, have become stunted, impotent, and in some cases extinct; yet it is said that seeds have lain dormant in arid soil for hundreds of years, to spring into leaf and flower as soon as the rains have fallen and the climate changed. The faculty of pure vision is like the latent seed-life. It waits only the conditions which favor its growth and development; and though for hundreds of years it may have lain dormant, yet in a few days, weeks, or months it may attain the proportions of a beautiful flower, a thing of wonder and delight, gracing the garden of the soul.

The Vision

Visions seen in the crystal are of two kinds, both of which may be conveyed to the perception of the seer in two ways. The two kinds of visions are direct visions and symbolic visions. The first of these is a representation of scene or incident exactly as it will transpire, or has already happened, either in relation to the seer, those sitting with him, or yet in relation to public affairs. The second order of vision is a representation, by means of symbol, ideograph, or other indirect means, of events similar to those conveyed by direct vision.

In most cases it will be found that answers to questions take the form of symbols. But this is not always so, as will appear from the following remarks concerning the manner in which these impressions or visions are conveyed to the perception of the seer.

The vision is conveyed in one of two ways-first, as a vivid picture affecting the focus and retina of the eye, perfect in its outline and coloring, and giving the impression of being either distant or near or at moderate range, Secondly, it may be conveyed as a vivid impression accompanied by a hazy and undefined formation in the crystal field. In this form it becomes an apperception rather than a perception, the consciousness receiving the impression of the vision to be conveyed before it has had time to form and define itself in the crystal.

The direct vision is more generally found in association with the passive type of seer. It is not usually as regular and constant as the symbolic vision, owing to the peculiarities of the negative temperament. When it does appear however, it is particularly lucid and actual, and has its literal fulfillment in the world of experience and fact. It is an actual representation of past or future event, or of what is then presently happening at some place more or less distant.

The symbolical vision is more closely associated with the positive temperament. It has the advantage of being more ready and constant in its manifestation than the direct vision, while on the other hand it is frequently a matter of speculation as to what the symbolic vision may portend.

The positive temperament, forceful in its action, appears to throw off the soul-images, afterwards going out towards them in a mood of speculative inquiry. The passive temperament, however, most frequently feels first and sees afterwards, the visionary process being wholly devoid of speculation or mental activity. The one sees and thinks, the other feels and sees, that is the distinction between the two temperaments.

In the early stages of development the crystal will begin to cloud over, first becoming dull, then suffused with milky clouds, among which sparkle a large number of little specks of light like gold dust in the sunlight. The focus of the eyes is inconstant, the pupil rapidly expanding and contracting, the crystal at times disappearing entirely in a haze or film which seems to pass before the eyes. Then the haze will disappear, and the crystal will loom up into full view again, accompanied by a lapse of the seer into full consciousness.

This may be the only experience of the first few sittings, it may be that of many; but, sooner or later, there will come a moment when the milky clouds and dancing star lights will suddenly vanish-a bright azure expanse like an open summer sky will occupy the field of vision; the brain will take up a spasmodic action, as if opening and shutting in the superior coronal region; there will be a tightening of the scalp on a level with the base of the brain, as if the floor of the cerebrum were contracting; the seer will catch his breath with a spasmodic sigh, and the first vision will stand out, clear and life-like, against the azure screen of heaven.

The danger at this supreme moment is that the seer will be surprised into full consciousness. During the process of abstraction which precedes every vision or series of visions, the consciousness of the seer is gradually and imperceptibly withdrawn from his surroundings. He forgets that he is seated in this or that room, that such a person is at his right hand, such another at his left. He forgets that he is gazing into the crystal. He hears nothing, sees nothing, save what is passing before the eyes of his soul. He loses sight, for the time, even of his own identity.

Therefore, when his vision is suddenly arrested by an apparition, startling in its reality and instantaneous production, even though hoped for and expected, the reaction is so violent and rapid that the seer is frequently carried back into the full consciousness of his physical conditions. Therefore, the qualifications of self-possession and confidence in one's own soul-faculties have been stated as of primary importance in this domain of research. Excess of joy or fear at sight of the vision will be fatal to its continuance and to the condition of mind required for the process of development. This fact must therefore be borne in mind.

Difficulties

We will cite a few of the obstacles to be met within the process of inducing the psychic vision, and some also which may be expected in connection with the faculty when induced.

Putting aside the greatest of all obstacles-that of constitutional unfitness-as having been already discussed, the first obstacle to be avoided is that of ill-health. The importance of a moderate and sustaining diet in regard to psychic development cannot be too strongly urged. All overloading of the stomach with indigestible food and addiction to alcoholic drinks tends to cloud the spiritual perception. It depletes the brain-centers, gives the heart too much work, and overthrows the equilibrium of the system. Ill-health follows; the mind is centered upon the suffering body, spiritual aspiration ceases, and the soul folds its wings and falls into the sleep of oblivion. The consciousness of man works from a center, which co-ordinates and includes all the phenomena of thought, feeling, and volition. This center of consciousness is capable of rapid displacement, alternating between the most external of our bodily functions and the most internal of our spiritual operations. It cannot be active in all parts of our complex constitution at one and the same moment. Hence it follows that when one part of our nature is active another is dormant as happens in sleeping and waking, dream-life being that wherein the center of consciousness hovers between the body and the soul.

With these considerations in mind it will be obvious to every one that a condition in which the consciousness is held in bondage by the infirmities of the body is not one conducive to psychic development. The constitution need not be robust, but it should at all events be free from disorder and pain. Some of the most ethereal natures are associated with a delicate organism, but while the balance is maintained the soul is free to develop its latent powers.

> **Editor's Note**: While no one can dispute the value of good health and a sensible diet, it should be noted that many of the greatest mediums and psychics in the past have not followed this, in fact, drug and alcohol abuse among this group has been very common.

It is advisable not to sit for crystal reading, or indeed for any order of psychic exercise, immediately after or before a meal. The body should be at rest and the mind contented and tranquil. Again, the attitude of the seer should not be too expectant or over-anxious in regard to the production of the vision. Let the development take its natural course. Do not force the young plant in its growth or it will come to a premature end. Take time, as nature does. It is a great work, and much patience is needed. The acorn becomes the sturdy oak only because nature is contented with small results, because she can afford to wait and is never in a hurry to see the result of its operations. Whoever breathes slowest will live the longest. This is an Eastern saying which voices a fundamental truth.

The vision is produced. The faculty of clairvoyance has become more or less under the control of the mind. New difficulties arise, and, of these, two will be conspicuous. The first is that of time-measure, and the other is that of interpretation. The former is peculiar to both orders of vision, the direct and the symbolic. The difficulty of interpretation is, of course, peculiar to the latter order of vision.

Time-measure is, perhaps, the greatest difficulty encountered by the seer. It is sometimes impossible to determine whether a vision relates to the past, the present, or the future. In most cases, however, the seer learns by experience how to distinguish, and frequently it will be found that an intuitive impression of the period involved comes with the vision itself. In our own experience the foreground, middle distance, and background, mark off the present, the approximate, and the distant future. In tracing the succession of events, we have found it convenient to think of time-measure at the outset, bending the sight upon, each month or year separately and in succession, noting the visions that arise with each in order. As regards the past or future, we distinguish between them by an intuitive sense rather than by any other means, and very rarely is this sense deceived, for it is part of the psychic faculty we had in training.

Therefore, if the vision appears in the foreground and, as it were, at the feet of the seer, then it may be taken as relating to the present or a quite recent date. In the same way, the middle distance indicates the near past or future, and the background denotes the more distant past or future. The other difficulty we have mentioned is that of interpretation of such symbols as may arise.

Symbols

Symbols are thought-forms which convey, by the association of ideas, a definite meaning in regard to the mind that generates them. They depend wholly upon the laws of thought, and the correspondence that exists between the spiritual and material worlds, between the subject and the object of our consciousness.

Among the ancients symbols were the original form of record, of communicating ideas, and of writing. The hieroglyphs of the Egyptians, the word-pictures of the aborigines of Central America, the ideographic writing of ancient Mongolia, are all forms of symbolic writing, drawn from natural objects. The Hebrew alphabet, the names of its 22 letters, clearly indicate the nomadic and simple life of those "dwellers in tents." Thus the names of the letters include such objects as ox, tent, tent-door, tent-peg, camel, fish, fish-hook, an eye, a hand, a basket, a rope-coil, a head, an ox-goad, water, etc. From the combination of these simple forms the words are constructed. Thus the word used to signify "knowledge" is derived from three letters, Yod, Daleth, Oin, which mean a hand, a door, and an eye. The hand denotes action, power, etc.; the door denotes entering, initiation, etc.; the eye denotes seeing, vision. Therefore the three ideographs, when combined, denote "opening the door to see," which is a very graphic way of conveying the idea of acquiring knowledge. One cannot help seeing the hand of the young Hebrew drawing aside the canvas door of the tent and peering in to see what secrets may be learned!

All symbols, therefore, may be translated by reference to the known nature, quality, and uses of the objects they represent. Thus a foot signifies a journey, and also understanding; a mouth denotes speech, revelation; an ear news, information, and, if ugly and distorted, scandal or abuse. The sun, shining brightly, denotes prosperity, honors. The moon, when crescent denotes success, increase, and improvement. The sun eclipsed shows death or ruin of a man; the moon, similarly afflicted, denotes equal danger to a woman. These are natural interpretations.

Every symbol, however, has a threefold interpretation, and the nature of the inquiry or the purpose for which the vision is sought must determine the meaning of the symbols. If they refer to the spiritual world the interpretation must be agreeable to the nature of the spirit, and similarly if they refer to the intellectual or physical worlds. Thus a pair of scales would denote Divine Justice in the spiritual sense, judgment in the intellectual sense, and obligation in the material sense. If the scales were evenly balanced the augury would be good. But if weighed down on one side it shows a corrupt judgment, a wrong conclusion, an unbalanced mind, failure in one's obligations, injustice, etc. And if a sword should lie across the scales or be seen overhead, then a speedy judgment will be meted out.

A ship is a symbol of intercourse, of trading, of voyaging, etc. If in full sail it shows that the communication with the spiritual world is increasing, that news from far-off lands will come to hand, that trade will increase, that a voyage will be taken. If aught is written on the sails it will be an additional source of enlightenment. If the ship's sails are drooping, then it denotes a falling away of spiritual influx of intelligence, and of trade. Expected news will not come.

Black bread denotes a famine, and if it be spotted with yellow blotches it shows a plague. This symbol was seen, with a goat butting at it, in June, 1896. There followed a famine and plague in India, which country is said to be ruled by the zodiacal sign Capricorn! The symbol was not deciphered till the event came to throw light upon it. In the same way a leaf of shamrock, denoting the Triple Alliance has been seen split down the center with a black line, denoting the fracture of the treaty. It would also seem to indicate that Ireland, whose symbol is the shamrock, will be separated by an autonomous government from the existing United Kingdom.

In similar manner all symbols arising in the crystal may be interpreted by reference to their known qualities and uses, as well as the associations existing between them and other things, persons, and places, in the mind of the seer. As we have already said, however, the meanings of most of the symbols will be conveyed to the consciousness of the trained seer at the time of their appearance in the crystal. Experience will correct many errors, and a symbol, once known, will assume a constant meaning with each seer, so that after repeated occurrence it will hold a definite signification.

It should be mentioned, however, that the same symbol will have different meanings with different seers. It is difficult to say why this is the case. But it probably arises from the difference of individual temperament. We have the same laws of thought and the same general constitution. Humanity holds us all within the bonds of a single nature. Yet, despite this fact, we have differences of opinion, of emotion, of sympathy and antipathy, of taste, and so forth. Therefore it would appear that the soul images projected by the magical power of the mind must have different significations with each of us, their interpretation being in some peculiar way in agreement with the nature of the person who sees them. As a result, no definite rule can be laid down as to interpretation, but it is advisable that the seer should be his or her own interpreter.

Thus, although every symbol has some general

signification in agreement with its natural qualities and uses, yet it obtains a particular signification in regard to each person. It is within common experience that this is the case in regard to dreams, wherein the faculty of seership is acting in its normal plane. Every person is a seer in dream-life, but few persons pay that attention to dreams that their origin and nature warrant. The crystal is but a means of bringing this normal faculty of dreaming into activity in the waking life. Yet, as stated above, the differences of import or meaning, even in the dream-world, of any particular symbol is a common experience. Thus one person will dream to be wading in water whenever there is trouble ahead. Another will dream of a naked child when similar troubles are about to occur, Butcher's meat will signify financial troubles to one person, to another a fortunate speculation.

Some Experiences

The following facts, in connection with predictions made from the crystal, have come to the knowledge of the writer, either as personal experiences or in association with others in which the faculty of clear vision is active.

A lady of title visited the seer in the month of June, 1896, and was told that she would hear news from abroad in some hot country concerning the birth of a child, a boy, who would arrive in the following year in the month of February. The lady did hear such news, and in February, 1897, a boy was born to the lady's sister in India. The same lady was told that on a certain date, while travelling, she would meet with an accident to the right leg. She fell between the platform and the footboard while getting into a train, and suffered severe abrasion of the right leg, together with a serious muscular strain which laid her up for several days. Previous to that the lady was to be surprised by some good fortune happening to her son in connection with papers and a contest. This happened at the time specified. Her son passed his examination for the military college with honors.

Mrs. H. was consulted by a lady of some ability in a special line of literature. This fact was not, however, within the knowledge of the seer. She was told that she would go up a certain staircase into a dingy room with a roll of something under her arm. She would see a dark man who was thick-set and of quiet demeanor. The man would take the roll, and it would be a source of good fortune to her at a later date.

The lady-consultant did so take a certain manuscript rolled up beneath her arm. She went up the dingy staircase described by the seer, and saw the man whose description had been given.

The manuscript was transferred from her hand to that of the publisher, for such was the man's occupation. The manuscript was accepted, and later on was published. So the prediction was literally fulfilled.

In the first case cited the vision was symbolical, and the interpretation was made by the seer himself. In the second case the vision was literal, and needed no interpretation. These two cases will serve for an illustration of the two types of vision.

Mrs. A. was consulted by a lady of the writer's acquaintance in 1893. She was told that she would not marry the person to whom she was then engaged, but would have to wait till a certain person, who was described, should come from a foreign country and take her away. This would happen; it was said, in the month of January, three years later. This event transpired in due course exactly as predicted, though nothing was further from the probable course of events; in fact, the lady was not a little irate at the allusion to the breaking off of her then existing relations, while the idea of marrying a person whom she had never seen, and for whom she could have no sort of regard, was naturally revolting to one so wholly absorbed as she was at the time.

Mrs. G. consulted the seer on September 27th, 1894. She was told she would have sickness incidental to the loins and shooting pains in the knees. [A figure was seen with a black cloth around the loins, the figure stooping and resting its hands upon its knees.] She would be the owner of a house in the month of December. [A house was seen covered with snow; the trees were bare.] A removal would be made when the trees were without leaf. [A bird was seen on a branch without leaf; the bird flies off.] The consultant would be engaged in a dispute concerning money. [Several hands seen grabbing at a pile of money.]

These events came to pass at the time predicted. It is advisable to note that in the first instance the symbolical vision is seen; in the second, a literal vision supervenes; and in the third and fourth cases the vision reverts to the symbolical. Here we have an instance of the overlapping of the two conditions of the temperament, the active and the passive state alternating.

As an illustration of the extreme difficulty of interpretation in the normal state of consciousness a symbol may be cited which was seen in the crystal for Miss X. "A shield, and a lion rampant thereon, in red." Now this might mean anything. It suggests the armorial bearings of a princely family. The lion rampant might mean the anger of a person in authority, as the lion is the avowed king of beasts. Its color, red, and its attitude are naturally expressive of anger. The shield might be a protection, though little needed by a lion, especially if the assailant were the fragile Miss X. to whom the vision had reference.

Now observe the interpretation of the seer. "You will hear news from a man of medium height and fair complexion concerning a foreign country. A letter will come in reference to something written by you which will be the very best thing that could happen. You will score a great success."

This interpretation, which is quite in line with the fact and which afterwards transpired, is probably as far removed from all that one might have expected as anything could well be. But we have to remember that the condition in which the seer voices the interpretation of symbols seen by him is a psychological one, and no doubt in that state natural symbols take on quite a different signification to that which they would hold in the normal state of waking consciousness.

How often do dreams have a marked influence upon the dreamer while still asleep; how often they assume proportions of magnitude and become pregnant with meaning to the dreamer, only to dissolve into ridiculous triviality and nonsense as soon as the person awakes! It would indeed appear that a complete hiatus exists between the visionary and the waking states of consciousness, so that even the laws of thought undergo a change when the center of consciousness is removed from the outer to the inner world of thought and feeling.

The writer has known cases of sickness predicted with remarkable accuracy, the time and the nature of the sickness being foretold with more or less accuracy. The reception of unexpected letters and telegrams; their import and consequences; the various changes, voyages, business negotiations and speculations occurring in the consultants' lives have been foretold by means of the crystal.

In one case a man was seen dressed in black and wearing the habit of a judge. He held some papers in his hands which he was endeavoring to conceal. He appeared unsuccessful in his efforts. A snake was seen at his feet. It rose up against him. A change took place in the field of the vision and the same man was seen lying on his death-bed. From this it was predicted that the man designated by the vision would be guilty of misrepresentation, and would be cut off by death three years from that time. The prediction was in every respect verified.

Not infrequently the visionary state is induced by excessive emotion, during which the prophetic faculty is considerably heightened. Some temperaments of a peculiarly sensitive order will fall into the clairvoyant condition while engaged in thought. The thread of thought is broken, and there appears a vision wholly unconnected with the subject but a moment ago in the mind. It would appear that the soul of the sensitive, while probing the depths of its inner consciousness, suddenly comes into contact with the thin partition which may be said to divide the outer world of thought and doubt from the inner world of intuition and direct perception, and, breaking through, emerges into the light beyond. The same may be said of cases which manifest the faculty of clear visions while in the hypnotic state, whether spontaneous or induced. The trance condition frequently manifests this faculty in conjunction with others, such as clairvoyance or clear-hearing and the sense of psychic touch.

Directions for using the spheres for crystal or mirror vision

Daylight and artificial light are both equally suitable. A north light is the best suited to the human eye.

Editor's Note: Most modern scryers agree that dim light is more conducive to entering the appropriate mental state for seeing visions.

Observer should sit back to the light, holding the crystal in the palm of the hand, which may rest comfortably on the lap, or it can be placed on a table with a stand under it, and a back screen of black velvet or dark material. The latter materially assists by cutting off side lights and reflections. Steady gazing in complete silence is absolutely necessary. Success depends chiefly upon idiosyncrasy or faculty in the gazers, for "Seers" are very often men and women of imperfect education, in fact they seem "born rather than made" but the faculty may be developed in many people, seemingly at first insensitive, by frequent short trials, say fifteen to twenty minutes at a time, or less if they get tired.

Success is indicated when the crystal, ceasing to reflect, becomes milky, a clouded color following (generally red, and its complementary green), turning to blackness, which seems to roll away like a curtain, disclosing to the view of the student, pictures, scenes, figures in action, sentences of warnings, advice, etc. Revival of latent or lapsed memory is one of the leading features of this experiment.

Some persons see at once, others after a time. Women see better than men visions of the past, present, and future, on the subjects upon which the mind feels anxious.

Editor's Note: It should be apparent to anyone who has read the rest of this book that I do not agree with everything in this abridgement of Dr. Old's book *"How to Read the Crystal"* but I decided to include his writings in this book because I found his examples and his explanation of symbolism interesting.

Appendix B - *"Crystal Gazing and Clairvoyance"*

Editor's Note: The following is an abridgement of the book *"Crystal Gazing and Clairvoyance"* by John Melville. This book was originally published in 1896 and the author describes the early beliefs regarding "magnetism" and the brain's ability to tap into the unconscious and the universal consciousness. This book primarily concerns the use of crystal balls rather than plain glass mirrors for scrying.

The name crystal is from the Greek word meaning "clear ice," or "frozen water." A crystal is a natural inorganic solid, bounded by plane surfaces, which are symmetrically arranged around certain imaginary lines called axes.

It was thought for many centuries that rock-crystal was water turned to stone, and this conception remained unchanged until the commencement of the seventeenth century. The term has since been rather loosely applied to any solid capable of assuming geometrical shape under the control of the natural laws; but the crystal which has ever found most favor for the purposes of "crystallomancy," or divination through the medium of "crystal gazing" is the beryl, a mineral (silicate of beryllia), which crystallizes in six-sided prisms, the sides of which are often striated longitudinally, but the terminating planes are usually, though not always, smooth. The precious stones known as aquamarine - sea green or sky-blue in color - the golden beryl, and the deep rich green known as the emerald, are all varieties of the beryl.

With an admixture of borax or soda, the beryl forms a beautiful clear glass. The "chrysoprasus" of the Scriptures (more green than ordinary beryl), and also the chrysoberylus (yellowed) and chrysolithus, which last was believed to be connected with sight, appear to have been names applied to different shades of Beryl.

The stone is called by the Italians, "beryl-crystal," but the English lapidaries drop the use of the latter word and simply call it "beryl." It expands by heat in a direction perpendicular to the principal axis, and contracts on the line of the axis; hence there is a point where the expansion and contraction exactly neutralize each other.

Beryl is harder than ordinary quartz.

It may be of interest to remark that Dr. J. Pell, an old writer, states that spectacles were originally made with the beryl-crystal, and that the Germans call a spectacle-glass "brill" (beryl) on that account.

The crystal-gazers in Ireland in the fifth century were known as the Specularii.

The name crystal was originally applied only to ordinary quartz, or "rock-crystal." Later on the term was more generally applied to any symmetrically formed mineral, solid, transparent, or opaque, contained or bounded by plane surfaces.

The colors of the beryl range from blue through honey-yellow to absolute transparency; the latter resulting from the presence of peroxide of iron, while the green and various shades of blue represent the effect of protoxide of iron in varying quantities. The favorite shade of this crystal by ancient Seers was the pale water-green beryl or delicate "aquamarine."

For the use of this hue, or tint, there appears to have been more than one reason. Certainly other stones such as the white sapphire, and even vessels of water, were pressed into service; but it must be remembered that water-green was, astrologically considered (and all divination was more or less connected with high astrology), a color especially under the influence of the Moon, an orb exerting very great magnetic influence.

Now, when we, in the first place, reflect that the beryl, emerald, sapphire, adamantine spar, etc., all contain oxide of iron, a substance presenting the strongest affinity for magnetism, and when we also remember that the strict injunctions of the ancient occultists to utilize the crystal only during the increase of the Moon, the idea naturally suggests itself that the connecting link between the crystal and the spiritual world is magnetism, attracted to and accumulated in or around the crystal by the iron infused throughout its constitution, and that the greater the increase of the Moon the greater consequently is the supply and accumulation of the lunar magnetism in the crystal.

But granted that the above mentioned theory be correct in relation to the crystal itself, the further question naturally arises - How is the operator placed en rapport with the crystal globe, sphere, or ovoid; or, in other words, what is the secret or modus operandi of bringing the inquirer or experimenter into direct contact with the crystal, and through its medium, with the unseen world?

To this question we render the following reply:

(a) By concentration in the crystal of the greatest possible influx of celestial or terrestrial magnetism, or both.

(b) By concentration in the body of the operator of unalloyed magnetism, through the purity of the amatory functions.

(c) By concentration of the mind, through the mental faculty of "concentrativeness," acting through the prenological brain "center," located in the superior portion of the first occipital convolution of the cerebrum.

Hence, those persons endowed with natural ability to concentrate the attention, are thereby aided in their use of the sphere.

(d) Concentration of the gaze upon the crystal. Why? Because, as taught by the famous Baron Reichenbach, there streams from the human eye an efflux of magnetism, projected from its reservoir in the cerebellum, when the gaze is concentrated upon a given point.

Editor's Note: We now know that there is no "efflux of magnetism" that projects out from the eyes.

At this juncture it may be remarked that the "centers" of sight are located by modern Phrenologists in the posterior lobes of the brain, above the region of the cerebellum.

Now observe:

(a) That the ancients taught the importance of strict purity in relation to the amatory nature, when either crystal-gazing, clairvoyance, or other occult efforts were put forth, and hence the use of boys and virgins in crystal-divination.

(b) That Phrenologists have located the propensity to physical love in the cerebellum, or small brain, just beneath the before mentioned posterior lobe of the cerebrum.

(c) This being so, the cerebellum became, as it were, a reservoir of magnetism, directly connected with the creative economy, or would at all events influence the quality of the magnetic outflow through the eyes - the brain "centers" for which lie just above the region of the cerebellum, as also does that area devoted to the "concentration of attention."

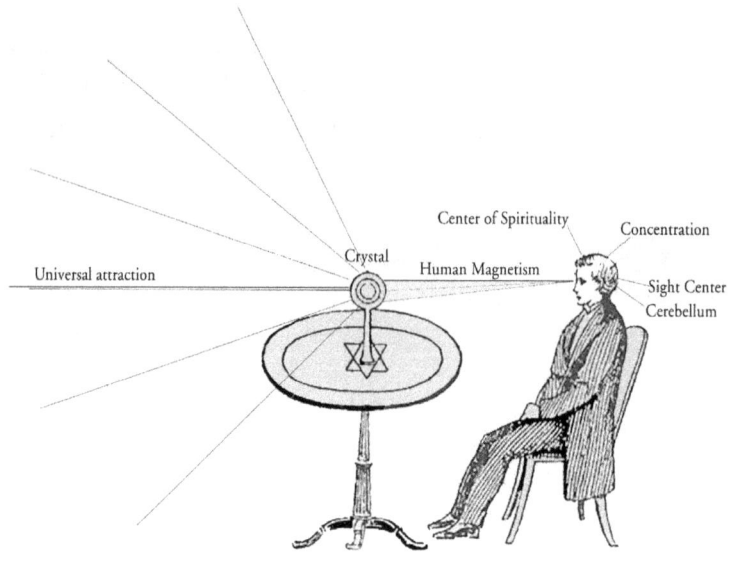

Melville's depiction of the "efflux" of magnetism

Purity of the blood is important to purity of power. Hence, the life fluid must be purified. Food, digestion, sleep, drinks - all must receive a proper degree of attention. Sound physical organs are not absolutely essential, but nevertheless it is best to enjoy healthy brain, heart, liver, kidneys, stomach, lungs, and pelvic apparatus, if one desires to attain to a high degree of lucidity, or clearness of mental vision, and all this largely depends as much upon air, light, diet, sleep, labor, music, health, as upon mechanically induced magnetism, or mesmerism.

Editor's Note: As I mentioned earlier in this book, history is filled with seers who were in anything but ideal physical condition. While no one disputes the value of good health and a sensible diet and exercise, I find it difficult to believe, given what I have seen, that this is a requirement for clairvoyance.

The condition of the vital fluid at the time of experimenting with the crystal being of so great importance, it will be of utility for the reader to consider the following facts:

There is, on an average, one part by weight of iron in two hundred and thirty human blood corpuscles, and the total quantity of iron in the blood of a man weighing one hundred and forty pounds, is about thirty-eight grains, while about one grain per day is on the average taken into the body with food. Iron is a component part of the hemoglobin of the blood, and forms the coloring matter of the red blood corpuscles. The white or colorless corpuscles which are much fewer in number than the red, in a healthy body are diminished by fasting, and increased by eating, and this fact is of interest in connection with the advisability of fasting prior to magnetic experiment with the crystal globe, as enjoyed by the Seers of the past.

Two principal forms of iron are apparent in the blood:

1. Protoxide of iron, which is principally found in the venous or dark blood. This is also known as ferrous oxide, and constitutes the base of the green or ferrous salts of iron, which latter cannot be obtained in an isolated state. Protoxide of iron combines with water to form a hydrate, FeO, HO, which, on the addition of an alkali, falls in white flakes, provided the water in which they are suspended contains no free oxygen; otherwise the precipitate is grey.

2. Peroxide of iron, which is mostly found in the

arterial, or bright scarlet blood. It is known as sesquioxide, or ferric oxide, "crocus of Mars," haemetite, or red oxide of iron. It is the base of the red or ferric salts (Fe_2O_2), and is practically the same thing as iron-rust, which is a hydrated peroxide.

Now, a compound of the two preceding oxides constitutes what was formerly known as the "loadstone," or black magnetic oxide of iron; and it is a remarkable fact that persons of dark or very dark hair, eyes, and skin are the most magnetic; and this darkness is, it would seem, connected with a preponderance of the protoxide of iron in the blood over the peroxide in the proportion of 2 parts to 1, which happens to be a similar proportion to that existing in the "loadstone."

Some of the iron is stored in the liver cells, and some discharged as phosphate into the bile, in which latter oxygen is almost wholly absent, though small quantities of nitrogen are found, the most important gas being the carbonic acid.

When we remember the importance of deep breathing in clairvoyant effort, the facts in general seem to point to the conclusion that a certain chemical balance between the ferric and oxygenic, and consequently magnetic conditions of the blood and bile, are necessary for obtaining the most perfect powers of concentration and lucid sight, or clairvoyance.

The phenomena of crystal vision may be classed as follows:

1) Images of something unconsciously observed. New reproductions, voluntary or spontaneous, and bringing no fresh knowledge to the mind.

2) Images of ideas unconsciously acquired from others, by telepathy or otherwise. Some memory or imaginative effect, which does not come from the gazer's ordinary self. Illustrations of thought.

3) Images, clairvoyant or prophetic. Pictures bringing information as to something past, present, or future which the gazer has no other chance of knowing.

I would impress upon the reader the fact that anything and everything perceived in the crystal does not belong to the phenomena coming under the third heading, which latter alone are in the category of true crystal-divination, as taught and practiced by the ancient Seers.

Such pictures as belong to divisions 1 and 2 may, of course, appear not only in a crystal, but in a vase, glass of water, etc., the mere result of visualization; and their production requires little or none of the care and observation of conditions herein set forth for the guidance of the more spiritual investigation.

Hints on the use of the crystal

1) Keep the crystal clean. If very dirty or discolored treat it as follows: Mix together six parts water and one part brandy. Boil them over a brisk fire, and let the crystal be kept in a boiling state about fifteen minutes. Then take out and rub carefully over with a brush dipped in the same liquor. Rub dry with chamois leather.

Editor's Note: I would be very reluctant to follow this advice if I owned an expensive crystal for fear of cracking it in the heat.

2) The person for whom you are going to look may hold it in their hands for a few minutes previous to its use, but no one else, except yourself.

3) If the crystal appears hazy or dull, it is a sign that you are about to see an image; it will afterwards clear, and the form or vision will manifest. Immediately before the apparition is beheld, the crystal becomes clouded or darkened, or what some term "black." Presently this clears away, and the crystal becomes exceedingly bright, as if illuminated by a light proceeding from its interior.

4) If you need to see events taking place at a great distance look lengthwise through the crystal.

The works of olden days insist upon elaborate ceremonial as follows:

a) Use frequent ablutions (washings) and prayers, three or four days before consulting the crystal.

b) The Moon must be in her increase, i.e., going towards the full. (This should never be neglected. It is of great importance to your success.)

c) When the Sun is in his greatest Northern declination is the best time, so far as regards his influence in the matter.

d) The room must be kept clean and neat, with nothing therein likely to disturb the attention, and should be kept locked when not in use.

e) The floor must be well scoured, or clean. Every preparation must be made during the Moon's increase.

f) Place in the room a small table, covered with a white linen cloth.

g) A chair, and materials for a fire. The fire is for burning the usual perfumes.

h) Two wax candles in gilt or brass candlesticks, highly polished.

The crystal should be about 1 ½ inches in diameter, or at least the size of a small orange. It should be enclosed in a frame of ivory, ebony, or boxwood, highly polished, or stood upon a glass or crystal pedestal.

When following strictly the ancient methods described herein, the crystal is to be stood upon the table, but if simply held in the hand, its top end should lean away from the gazer, and should be held so that no reflections or shadows appear therein. If stood on the table, the folds of a black silk handkerchief may be arranged about the crystal so as to shut out reflections.

No crystal or mirror should be handled by other than the owner, because such handling mixes the magnetisms and tends to destroy their sensitiveness. Others may look into them, but should not touch them, except the person who may be consulting the gazer, as already mentioned.

If the surface becomes dirty or soiled, it may be cleaned with fine soapsuds, rinsed well, washed with alcohol or vinegar and water, and then polished with soft velvet or chamois leather.

> **Editor's Note:** This seems to contradict the author's previous cleaning instructions, but this method makes more sense to me.

The crystal or mirror should frequently be magnetized by passes made with the right hand for about five minutes at a time. This aids to give it strength and power. Similar passes with the left hand add to the sensitiveness of the crystal.

The back of the mirror or crystal should be held toward the light, but its face never.

Moon light benefits the mirror or the crystal while direct sunlight will ruin the magnetic susceptibility of the crystal.

The magnetism with which the surface of the mirror or crystal becomes charged, collects there from the eyes of the gazer, and from the universal ether, the brain being as it were switched on to the Universe, the crystal being the medium.

Persons of a "magnetic temperament," such as those who are classified as brunette, dark-eyed, brown-skinned, and having dark hair, will charge the crystal or mirror quicker, but not more effectively, than those of opposite or eclectic temperament, such as the blonde.

Persons of the male sex are not so easily developed into seership as the female, but become exceedingly powerful and correct when they do so.

Among women, virgins see best, and next to them in

order widows.

In all cases boys and girls, before puberty, make the quickest and sharpest seers. This is because their magnetism is unmixed, unsexed; and purity gives power in all magnetic and occult experiments.

> **Editor's Note:** It is now believed that children are clairvoyant because they have not yet learned to censor what they see. But as I mentioned earlier in this book, it is no longer deemed to be appropriate to use children as seers.

Warning

A sure and certain law exists, that if the seer's purpose be evil when he or she uses the crystal or mirror, it will react upon the seer sooner or later with terrible effect; wherefore all are strictly cautioned to be good and do good only.

The aerial spaces are thronged with countless intelligences - celestial, good, pure, true, and the reverse. To reach the good ones, the heart of the gazer must correspond, and they should be invoked with prayerful feelings.

Appearances in the crystal

White clouds	=	good, the affirmative, favor
Black clouds	=	bad, inauspicious
Violet, green, blue	=	coming joy, excellent outcomes
Red, orange, yellow	=	danger, trouble, sickness, deception, loss
Ascending clouds	=	yes, affirmative replies to questions
Descending clouds	=	no, negative replies to questions

• Whatever appears on the **left-hand side** of the gazer is real, or a picture of an actual thing.

• Whatever appears on the **right-hand side** of the gazer is symbolic.

• Clouds or shadows moving toward the gazer's right hand indicate the presence of spiritual beings and their interest.

• Clouds or shadows moving toward the gazer's left hand indicate that the séance is ended for the present time.

Appendix C - "Hygienic Clairvoyance"

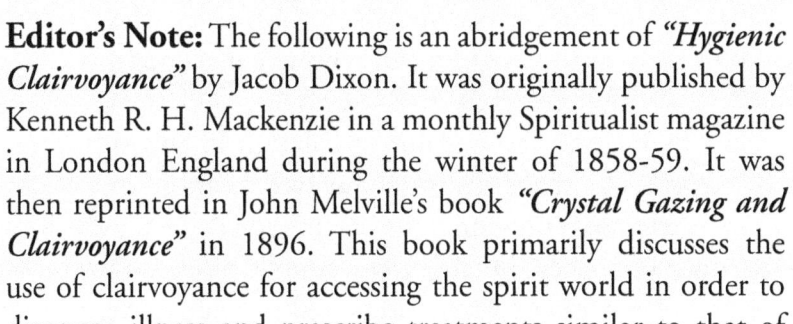

Editor's Note: The following is an abridgement of *"Hygienic Clairvoyance"* by Jacob Dixon. It was originally published by Kenneth R. H. Mackenzie in a monthly Spiritualist magazine in London England during the winter of 1858-59. It was then reprinted in John Melville's book *"Crystal Gazing and Clairvoyance"* in 1896. This book primarily discusses the use of clairvoyance for accessing the spirit world in order to diagnose illness and prescribe treatments similar to that of famed 20th century American psychic Edgar Cayce.

In this text there is a lot of discussion about Mesmerism and Phrenology which is now outdated. We understand much more about the workings of the brain and in particular of hypnotism now than was known in the mid 1800's but I decided to include this information in this book because the author explains what was historically believed regarding clairvoyance and contact with the spirit world.

Introduction

The subject of hygienic clairvoyance, however novel it may appear to modern readers, is not new to the world.

The ancient Grecian philosophers, Pythagoras and Plato, and their successors, who discoursed of hygiene as a department of human wisdom, had recourse to clairvoyance - the clear sight of the magnetic sleep.

They regarded the clairvoyant, or clear-see-er, as a living entrance door to the sacred temple of inner realities. They knew that to such a one the internal becomes, without the use of the other senses, more perceptible than the external is to us by the ordinary mode of objective perception.

Pythagoras received his instruction in this subject in the temples of Egypt, in which, as well as those of ancient India, there are representations of individuals being put into the magnetic sleep by the same simple process which we moderns have, of late years, discovered to be effective.

The family of Hippocrates were ministers in the temple of Aesculapius. Hippocrates' knowledge of clairvoyance is shown by the following passage in his writings:

"The sight being closed to the external, the soul perceives truly the affections of the body."

This exactly states the case of the clairvoyant. He used to treat some disorders by the application of the hands; in other words, he used to magnetize - or as we in those days would say, mesmerize - the patient, probably under clairvoyant indications.

Pythagoras himself used this means to procure quiet sleep, with good and prophetic dreams. He even says that the art of medicine originated in this divine sleep.

Aesculapius is said, according to Cicero, who wrote on this subject, to have uttered oracles in the temple sleep, for the cure of the sick.

If we turn to the sacred Scriptures, we there learn many things in relation to this subject. Moses, it may be inferred, with other lore of the Egyptians, was instructed by their wise men in this magnetic science. We read of a youth being restored to life by prophet; of an angel indicating the means of Tobias recovering his sight, etc.

The Jewish philosophic sect, the Essenes, it is matter of history, also taught the system, and practiced it, of healing by "laying on of hands." It may be inferred that they knew also of hygienic clairvoyance, which is but an advanced chapter out of the same book.

The Romans, who received their philosophy from Greece, could not but be acquainted with this department of it; and so we read without surprise that, with them as with the Greeks, the sick used to be brought to the temples, where remedies were revealed by this means for their disorders.

The Sibyls -- virgin prophetesses of the Temple of Jupiter; clairvoyants under care of the priests of the temple -- according to St. Justin, declared many true things, and when the intelligence which animated them was withdrawn, remembered nothing of what they had said. This describes clairvoyance.

> **Editor's Note:** Dixon's description of the activity performed by ths Sibyls more acurately describes trance mediumship than clairvoyance. Claivoyance does not require that another intelligence takes over the person, and it generally does not involve not remembering what took place.

A century before Mesmer's discovery, Van Helmont wrote: "Magnetism is in action everywhere; there is nothing new in it but the name; it is a paradox, strange and fantastical, only to those who are skeptical of everything, or who attribute to the power of the Devil that which they themselves cannot render account of."

It is to the resuscitation of magnetic science, under the auspices of Mesmer and his school, that the revival of the philosophic study and application of hygienic clairvoyance is due. It is this school which furnishes modern testimony, abundant and varied, to the value and importance of our subject.

The advocates of Mesmeric science having established for it an acknowledgement of its applicability in numerous disorders.

> **Editor's Note:** Franz Anton Mesmer (1734 -1815), was a German physician and astrologer, who developed a form of medical treatment based on what he called animal magnetism, which involved the use of magnets and the laying on of hands to cure patients of various illnesses. His theories became known as "mesmerism." Scottish surgeon James Braid later refined Mesmer's ideas in order to develop hypnosis in 1842.

Clairvoyance: Its Theory and Practice

In the course of curing by Mesmerism, some patients pass into an extraordinary state, which modern physiologists call an "abnormal" one and which state is variously divided by careful observers into certain ascending degrees.

"As the patient advances in these degrees," says one of these observers (Kluge, of Berlin), *"so does he seem to recede from the sensuous world."*

This state, however, even in its lowest degree, cannot be induced in all patients; nor is an ascent to the highest degree necessary for the recovery of health, for many patients remain only in the lowest degree during the whole of their Mesmeric treatment up to their complete cure. Some become more and more influenced by every succeeding operation, progressively ascending to the highest; others pass to the highest at once, and continue in it, whenever operated upon, to the end of their cure.

"In the first degree," continues Kluge, *"the usual channels of access by which the soul communicates with the external world remain open; external sensation being intact, the subject perceives himself still in the ordinary sphere of things: this I call the:*

1) **Waking degree**.

2) **Half sleep.** In it the eyes are closed, but the other senses are not entirely sealed.

3) **Magnetic sleep.** In which the patient is as if stupefied; but while thus standing, as it were, upon the

verge of the world of sense, he still retains the recollection of actual or sensuous life.

4) **Somnambulism.** (Sleep-walking.) This degree is distinguishable from the preceding by the presence of consciousness.

5) **Self-inspection.** (Introvision.) In this degree the patient obtains a luminous knowledge of the interior state of his body and mind, diagnoses his complaint, and indicates the most effectual remedies for its cure.

6) **Clairvoyance.** In the sixth degree, the patient passes out of the bounds of his own physical body and enters into rapport, or relation, with objects in universal nature; the faculty of Introvision becomes exalted into that of Extrovision (clairvoyance), extending to and into objects and individualities, near and remote, in space and time.

Thus far I agree with Kluge. He goes on to say that in this degree the patient becomes abstracted from all things mean and terrestrial, and is exalted to the grandest and noblest sentiment; he undergoes a transmutation of being; a spirit speaks through him, etc. But, this extra elevation above clairvoyance clearly marks a seventh degree - that of Extasis, or trance, the degree in which there is interior relation with the individualities and objects of the spiritual world.

This, however, merely in passing, for we have nothing to do at present with the subject of extasis - we pause at that of clairvoyance, that degree of the state in which the subject transcends the bounds of his own physical body and is able to enter into immediate rapport with external objects and individuals of this world.

With this definition of the faculty of clairvoyance it will next be for us to consider some instances of it in exercise.

Before doing this let us dwell a little upon the belief that the faculty in question is "abnormal," "morbid," more especially in cases where it occurs spontaneously.

Man possesses not only the faculties of external perception and reason, but those of internal perception, of intuition and instinct of a higher degree, corresponding to the intuition and instinct of all animated beings, and which are as serviceable to the species as is his observation of things by the external senses.

Through instinct, animals move from place to place, from region to region, and distinguish wholesome from noxious plants. By the same faculties in man, did he not, in the early times of the race, discover the qualities of many of our traditional medicines? In those early times those interior faculties seem to have been more active than that of reason; while in the times approaching our own, the faculty of reason has borne sway and been more fostered.

Nevertheless, the intuitive and instinctive faculties, being as innate in man as in all animals, have ever been stronger or weaker, more or less active, guides of the race. The records of their activity appear only sparsely and obscurely in the annals of European civilization - the culminating characteristic of which has been the cultivation of the sensuous and the rational.

Psychologists, with Kluge, infer from all its phenomena that clairvoyance is a faculty common to humanity, but exercised by the being when in a certain state, which occurs spontaneously, but which may be induced by various agencies and means; that in this state the soul which perceives is more or less freed from its body; that the state is therefore a psychical or spiritual state.

Within the last few years the records of this faculty of clairvoyance, spontaneous and induced, have been numerous.

> **Editor's Note:** Here the author is making reference to the beginnings of the Spiritualist movement where examples of clairvoyance and Spirit contact began popping up around the world.

Although it is denied that clairvoyance is a symptom of disorder, in as much as it presents itself in normal health, yet it is readily granted that it frequently presents itself where the subjects, always of the nervous temperament, have suffered from illness. But indeed clairvoyance presents itself in subjects in all states of health; verified instances of this are abundant enough to fill volumes.

It is painful sometimes to contemplate the straining of some of our philosophers in their efforts to debase every mental manifestation, above sensuous perception, into a symptom of organic disorder. With such philosophers genius would stand as delirium, poetry as insanity, inspiration as illusion, bringing their subjects properly under the treatment of the doctor and druggist.

But the faculty, like other faculties, may be too continuously exercised. Look at other clairvoyants, in whom organic health has been almost undisturbed since they have regularly exercised this faculty, and it must be agreed that there is no connection necessarily between the questions of clairvoyance and health. Indeed, ill health operates against the exercise of the faculty in those in whom it is developed. The clairvoyant of the greatest lucidity I have ever known, in questions connected with health, on one occasion, when her health had received a shock from some sudden excitement, was not able to pass into the state even of Introvision until she was convalescent; nor could she resume her clairvoyant examinations until she had regained her ordinary good health.

The psychological or spiritual school holds that every being and naturally formed object is, in its beginning, a spiritual or monadial entity; that having its origin in, it must necessarily have continuous relations with, the spiritual or monodial plane of existence, as well as with the material or sensuous plane in which it is made to develop itself; that each, according to species, etc., evolves from its monadial center an essential aura, which has positive and negative magnetic relations with the essential aura of every other.

Mesmeric attraction and repulsion exhibit a strong analogy with magnetic attraction and repulsion. Analogous attraction and repulsion exists, not only between individuals of the same, but of different species, and not only in animate beings, but in inanimate nature.

A few words at this point may not be amiss, with respect to the intervention of spirits in the phenomena under examination.

In the first place, let us keep in mind that we, in the material or earthly body, are as much spirits as those who have vacated this mortal frame.

Secondly, that clairvoyance is thus a faculty, exercised by a human spirit clothed in a body.

Thirdly, that the body of the subject should ever be in health for the exercise of the lucid faculty.

Fourthly, that, as is well known, the faculty in any individual, like other faculties, is strengthened by the regular and reasonable exercise of it.

Fifthly, that the faculty is of a prominently hereditary character in some families.

> **Editor's Note:** Anyone who has read the rest of this book, or any of my other books knows that I vehemently disagree with the idea that mediumship/clairvoyance has a hereditary component. I believe that it is a natural human ability that each of us share. The reason why it appears to run in families is because if you have other family members who use their pyschic abilities then you are more likely to recognize these abilities in yourself. Belief in the concept of an inherited psychic aristocracy leaves the rest of us at the mercy of the few when it comes to getting messages from loved ones on the "other side."

Keeping these several points in mind, we cannot help recognizing in clairvoyance an undoubted exercise of the individual's own faculty and powers of perception - spiritual, and at the same time natural. Of this exercise, we find more or less perfect examples in proportion to the more or less complete detachment from the sensuous plane.

Ancient philosophy recognized a reciprocal influence among all entities; between the earth and all the naturally formed things and beings on it, and between these and the sun, moon, planets, stars - the visible bodies of the macrocosm. It also included among entities, invisible or spiritual beings, under various names, to whom it accorded a greater or lesser influence among the entities of the earth. The foundations of this philosophy were laid by seers, prophets, oracles - those who were pre-eminently subject of the divine sleep, the trance. Upon the breaking up of ancient civilization the philosophy disappeared, except so much as was, in its spiritual part, purified in the Christian religion.

In the early Christian church the influence and action of spiritual beings, for the purposes of health (as, for instance, in the Bible story of the troubling of the waters of a certain pool by an angelic being), were as much acknowledged by worshippers as in the temples of their ancestors. This acknowledgement is still made by some sects of the church, and doubtless whatever individual opinion may be held regarding the general tenets of Roman Catholicism, its recognition of spiritual or angelic ministrations, represents the truth concerning this matter. But when literary Europe accepted the canons of criticism laid down by Hume and Voltaire, all this was gradually and erroneously set down as bygone superstition, and it was held that everything not sensuously present (able to be physically seen) was - in all future time - to be treated as non-existent. A greater delusion was never promulgated; yet such was the effect of this materialistic teaching that men have, even to the present time, deliberately closed their eyes against the truth, and at the end of the 19th century are still floundering in the darkness which they have fondly attributed to the past.

Even the medical profession has for many years flouted and opposed the truths of Mesmerism, to such an extent indeed that even men of their own colleges - such, for instance, as the famous Dr. John Elliotson who was in recent years hounded to death in London for his noble and daring advocacy of Phrenology and Mesmerism. Only now is the truth once more dawning, and under the name of hypnotism a force long opposed is being gradually accepted and applied by such men as Prof. Charcot, Dr. Lloyd Tuckey, and others.

Editor's Note: Phrenology (from the Greek words for "mind"; and "knowledge") was developed by German physician Franz Joseph Gall in 1796 and was influential in 19th century psychiatry and neuroscience.

The theory of Phrenology is based on the concept that the brain is the organ of the mind, and that each area of the brain is responsible for specific functions. It was believed that the areas of the brain developed according to an individual's particular abilities, and that the cranial bones grew to accommodate brain development in each area. Therefore a person's capacity for a particular trait could be determined by measuring the area of the skull that overlies the corresponding area of the brain.

While it has been proven that different parts of the brain are indeed responsible for various mental functions, the idea that you can determine personality traits or intelligence by the size and shape of the skull has been disproven.

Literature and criticism were in the before-mentioned condition when Mesmer revived a part of the old philosophy, the reciprocal influence of all visible entities. He demonstrated that a correspondent property to that of polarity and inclination in the loadstone was possessed by man and other beings. To this magnetism he applied the name of "animal"-- to distinguish it in use from the mineral kind. Tracing disturbance of health in many cases to disturbance of magnetic polarity, he and his followers showed that by restoring polarity health might be frequently restored. Patients treated by magnetism sometimes pass into a new state. This state was found to be divisible into various degrees.

In the ultimate degrees of this state the patient passes the bounds of his physical body and enters into a rapport with other objects and individualities, near and remote in space and time - these are clairvoyance and trance.

The brain-system is the focal apparatus of sensation and will. The ganglionic that of intuition, instinct, and sympathy. Facts demonstrate that these apparatuses are the immediate concrete instruments of the soul, by which it has polar organic relations with the material sphere, and thus on the natural plane is made to move spiritual man, who - through the soul - has polar relations also with the spiritual sphere, as manifested in the phenomena of clairvoyance and trance.

In clairvoyance, and in trance especially, we witness a passing from activity on the external plane of conscious being to that on an internal; in other words, the essential being is polarized from the natural to the spiritual plane; the vito-magnetic currents ceasing, more or less, to circulate through the external nerves, few impressions, or none, are transmitted from without to the brain, but to the organic seat of instinct and intuition. In most subjects the perceptive powers, are intensified, and there is, with clear sight of mundane individualities, spiritual clairvoyance and clairaudience. The degree of change thus effected by this spiritual polarization is determined by the idiosyncrasy of the subject; but that, with the will of the operator, and circumstantial conditions, has also to be taken into account.

Under some operators subjects will exhibit only the phenomena of mundane clairvoyance, while under others they will seem to exhibit the illumination of ancient seership. This change in the direction of the vito-magnetic forces of the soul, may be induced in sensitive subjects, not only by the magnetic process, but also by the day's exhaustion of sensibility, irritability, and will; by various drugs, or by wish or passivity, reciprocating, consciously or unconsciously, with the action of another, visible or invisible.

Summary

In the course of my observations, I have noticed incidentally the fact that clairvoyance and clairaudience are sometimes induced by spiritual operation. The subjects of this kind of clairvoyance are called ecstatics.

However, clairvoyance is sometimes remotely induced by the operation of natural objects. Koener, Richenbach, Ashburner - his annotator - and others, have demonstrated that some subjects have their normal polarity disturbed, more or less completely inverted, by the action of natural objects upon them.

Clairvoyance, embraced by physical science, and properly induced by medical art by various means, but chief of all by human magnetism, is the department which, as hygienic clairvoyance, falls naturally within the province of the physician. This faculty, enabling the perceiving soul to come, while still in the body, into rapport with the inner forms, qualities, and states of other beings, and temporal things, enables the physician to investigate all natural objects for hygienic purposes.

In saying this nothing hypothetical or doubtful is declared. The faculty, employed from the earliest ages, has been used for years past by very many of note, for the intuitive perception of diseases, remedies, and antidotes; in the discerning of which, the subject in the clairvoyant state is monadially or spiritually affected by the monadial or spiritual properties of the objects under examination.

The distinctive advantages presented by the employment of hygienic clairvoyance, to the patient and the physician, are:

1st. Exactness of diagnosis in exploring the seat of any internal disorder, and in obviating the employment of the doubtful stethoscope, the objectionable speculum, etc.

2nd. The exact discrimination of temperament and constitutional peculiarity, and correspondingly exact adaptation of medicine and dose.

3rd. Exact appreciation of the moral state and its condition as cause or consequence of the physical disorder.

4th. The subjective symptoms - those felt only by the patient - becoming objective to the physician through the clairvoyant's perception.

These are advantages which cannot but be appreciated; and not more by the patient than by the honest physician. For how often is he not obliged to confess that ordinary discrimination is at fault? We all know that the most acute physicians err sometimes in their diagnosis even when aided by the best contrivances invented by ingenuity; and where there is error in diagnosis there is necessarily error in treatment.

How often do we meet with cases where, from inevitable error of diagnosis, a system of mere palliation has been prescribed on the ground of impossibility of cure.

Such are the cases against which, under divine providence, the physician can successfully cope by the light and aid of hygienic clairvoyance.

> **Editor's Note:** I think it is very unlikely that many modern doctors would be willing to attempt to make diagnoses in this manner, I'm pretty sure that would invalidate their malpractice insurance, and it is definitely wrong for a lay person to attempt to diagnose medical problems and suggest treatments by any method. However, if you are attempting to diagnose and treat your own medical issues why not give it a try as long as you back up your findings with proper medical care.

Magnetic Clairvoyance

Magnetic clairvoyance may be induced by holding the head close to the open horns of a large and powerful horseshoe magnet. It may be suspended from the ceiling, and held to the head lying down, so that when let go it will spring away, so as to close the circuit. A quartz crystal is almost as good as a horseshoe magnet for the foregoing purpose.

> **Editor's Note:** I would be very hesitant about suspending a large magnet from the ceiling and letting it swing away from my head for obvious reasons, but I do find it interesting that the author states that a quartz crystal is almost as good as a magnet for inducing clairvoyance.

All clairvoyants should, to be useful, successful, and enduring, cultivate the habit of deep breathing, for all brainpower depends largely upon lung power. Continued ability cannot exist if deep breathing is neglected.

All clairvoyants should feed on the best things obtainable.

Clairvoyants must exercise great caution in matters relevant to the procreative functions. Abstinence in this direction is good, and total abstinence is still better. An error in this direction is fatal to clear vision, and may cause a lengthened suspension of power.

> **Editor's Note:** Hmmm, I feel that I have to comment on this. I am happily married and a failure to follow this author's admonishments regarding abstinence has not had any detrimental effect on my ability to go into an altered state and see visions.

Rapid breathing, forcibly, for ninety seconds, while lying down, in connection with the horseshoe magnet operation, will prove successful in enabling you to see without eyes if you are a good subject.

All magnetic, odyllic, and mesemeric processes are 20 times more productive of successful results if conducted in:

1) A dark room.

2) Next to a perfectly dark room, moonlight or starlight is preferable.

A successful method of inducing clairvoyance

1) Room partly darkened.

2) Mirror in the north end.

3) Subject sits with back turned toward the mirror.

4) Operator (magnetizer), subject, and mirror should form a triangle.

5) The subject sits so that the reflected ray of light (magnetism), from the operators eye, will strike the back of his or her head - the subject receiving the reflected ray.

6) The subject is to be seated in a chair having all its legs fully insulated and having his or her feet resting on an insulated stool.

7) No part of the subject's clothing, or the chair must touch the floor.

8) Not a soul must be in the north end of the room.

9) Any other person present must remain quietly seated in the south, east, or west portion of the room.

10) No silk (not even a cravat or a ribbon) must be present in the room.

11) One soft and gentle chord may be played on the piano, but no other on the same evening.

12) Previous to the experiment, two magnets should be suspended - one with the north pole up, the other with the north pole down, so as to embrace the subject's head without much pressure.

13) The operator now takes a prepared bar magnet in his hand, and fixing his gaze steadily on that point of the looking glass from when the reflected ray will glance off and strike the back of the subject's head, just between the fork of the northern magnet he points the bar magnet directly towards the open neck of the subject. In a few minutes there should be absolute magnetic slumber induced in the subject, who will then frequently exhibit the most remarkable powers of clairvoyance.

Editor's Note: We know now that hypnotism is not dependent on the use of magnets, but this setup probably helped both the "subject" and the "operator" to enter the hypnotic state through the use of ritual. We now know that staring at a fixed point in a

> darkened room, combined with rapid breathing helps to induce an altered state. Readers might be interested in experimenting with setting up the directions of the chairs and the mirror in the reading room.

In seeking to become clairvoyant

Food – Daily diet should be very light. Fruit, tea, coffee, milk, may be freely used, but no chocolate, fat, oysters, or pastry, and very little sugar.

Fasting - Strict fasting for at least 24 hours before using the crystal is advantageous to the success of the experimenter.

Skin, head, hair - Must be kept scrupulously clean. The bath is the very best preparation for experiments and no one can reach good results unless perfectly and absolutely clean.

Patience - Is a most necessary qualification.

Silence - Perfect stillness should be observed when using the crystal.

Time - Usually allow 10 - 15 minutes for attaining a crystal vision. In some cases 1 or 2 hours have been known to elapse before any result was obtained.

What is the difference between:

        A) Clairvoyance
        B) Psychometry
        C) Intuition

Answer:

        A) Clairvoyance **sees**, more or less distinctly.
        B) Psychometry **feels**, with greater or lesser intensity.
        C) Intuition **knows** - leaps at results at a single bound.

Clairvoyance depends upon a peculiar condition of the brain and nerves. It is compatible with the most robust health, though sometimes the accompaniment of disordered nerves.

What proportion of persons can become clairvoyant?

As a broad rule 75 out of 100 can become partly lucid.

    63 in 100 can become "sensitives."
    45 in 100 can reach the second degree of clairvoyance
    32 in 100 can reach the third degree of clairvoyance
    14 in 100 can reach the fourth degree of clairvoyance
    5 in 100 can reach the fifth degree of clairvoyance
    2 in 100 can reach the sixth degree of clairvoyance

Of 100 men, 56 can become seers.
Of 200 women, 180 can become seers.

Editor's Note: I can't stress this enough, I disagree with Dixon's conclusions. I think that anyone who has an interest in this subject and who has a desire to learn can develop clairvoyance.

*"There are more things
in heaven and earth, Horatio,
Than are dreamt of in your philosophy."*

William Shakespeare

Index

A

abstinence 175
acrylic paint 62-68
Aesculapius 161
affair of the diamond necklace 19
Akashic Records 52
alchemy 16, 18
alcohol 86-87, 98
ancient Greece 11, 74
ancient Persia 12
angelic language 17
angels 1, 13, 16-17, 30-33, 45, 57
Antoinette, Marie 19
apothecary 14
archetypes 53-54, 92
asperging 81
astral plane 8, 56, 61, 79
astral projection 2
astrologers 47
atomic bomb 15
Avignon 14

B

Balsamo, Giuseppi 18-20
Barrett 123
beryl crystal 61, 71, 120-121, 127, 146-147
besom 80
Bible 2, 12, 46-47, 161, 169
black construction paper 62, 67, 68
black magic 72
black paint 62-68
Blavatsky, Helena 119
blessing the mirror 68-69
Boehme, Jacob 121
boiling oil 13
Bonaparte, Napoleon 15
Bond, James 15
bowl of water 7, 14, 70, 83, 89, 92, 121
Braid, James 162
British Museum 16
broom 80
Buddhism 108

C

cabinet 74
caffeine 97
Cagliostro, Count 18-20
campfire 7
candles 7, 85, 89, 93, 94
Catholic Church 14, 18
Cayce, Edgar 159
celebrity psychic 104
Celts 11
censoring mind 103-104
cerebellum 149
charlatans 104
children 19, 41-44, 103, 157
Christianity 2, 12, 46-47, 169
Church of Jesus Christ of Latter Day Saints 20
clairvoyance 71, 159-179
clear crystal 72
cloud formations 24, 95, 130
collective unconscious 52
concentration 3
conscious mind 3, 8, 95, 108
construction paper 62, 67
craft paint 62-68
creativity 2, 98
crystal 120-121, 126, 143, 145-147
crystal balls 7, 61, 71-74, 92, 120-121, 126, 143-147

crystal bowl 92
Crystal Gazing and Clairvoyance 70, 145
crystallomancy 146
Cup of Jamshid 12

Essenes 161
ethereal plane 79
evil spirits 57-58, 59
Exodus 46

D

danger 41-44
Daniel 47
darkened mirror 1, 6, 11, 23
daydreaming 4
deceased loved ones 1, 3, 4, 6, 28, 30, 45, 84, 96, 114
decreasing phase of the moon 94
Dee, Dr. John 15-18, 105
Delphi 105
demons 2
Deuteronomy 46
dimensions 8
divination 46, 146
Dixon, Jacob 101, 159
dogs 26
doorway 9
dreams 141
driving a car 48-49

E

Edinburgh 21
Edison, Thomas 33-34
efflux of magnetism
Egypt 18, 135, 160, 161
Elizabethan England 15-18
energy 55
England 15-18
Enochian language 17
Ephyra 74

F

fasting 86
Ford, Henry 33, 103
forensic accountant 102
forger 16
Fortress of San Leo 19
France 13-15, 18
Franklin, Benjamin 18, 31-32
fraud 104
Freemason 19
French Revolution 15
Freud, Sigmund 47-48

G

Galatians 46
Genesis 12, 46
German Shepherd 26
ghosts 9
glass cleaner 68
God 12, 44-45, 52
Greece 11, 16, 39, 74, 161
Greek mythology 39
Gretsky, Wayne 105
gut feelings 102
gypsies 7, 72

H

Halloween 20
hallucinations 2, 9, 94
Hawaiian Islands 12
herbal remedies 14, 15
heredity 168
heresy 19
higher power 83-84
Hill, Napoleon 31-32
Hippocrates 160
Hiroshima 15
Hitler, Adolf 15
holy water 81
How to Read the Crystal 119-144
hunches 102
Hygienic Clairvoyance 101, 159
hypnotism 19, 159

I

incense 7, 11, 84, 93
increasing phase of the moon 94
India 108, 160
Infinite Spirit 83-84
Inquisition, the 19
intention 29-38, 96
internal dialogue 27
intuition 102
inventors 2
Italy 14, 18-20

J

Jesus 57
Joseph 12, 46-47
Judaism 161
Jung, Carl 52, 54
Justine, St. 161

K

Kabala 18
Kahuna 12
Kelly, Edward 16-18
Kennedy, John F. 15

L

Latin 16
layers of reality 55-56
Leviticus 46
Lily Dale, NY 106
Lincoln, Abraham 21, 31
Lincoln, Mary 21
lost objects 33

M

MacKenzie, Kenneth 13, 105
magic 15, 16, 18, 23, 87
magicians 47
magnetic clairvoyance 174, 175
magnetic energy 70-71
magnetism 120, 126, 145, 147-149, 160, 162-163

malevolent entities 57-58
Malta 18
Maoris 11
meditation music 89, 91
mediumship 1, 24
Melville, John 70, 145, 159
Mesmer, Frans Anton 162, 171
Mesmerism 70-71, 159, 162, 163, 170
metaphors 38
metaphysical studies 16
middle realm 9, 56
missing persons 2, 33
missionaries 12
monkey mind 108
Moody, Dr. Raymond 74
moon 93-94, 147, 154
moonlight 156
Mormons 20
Moses 161
music 85, 89

N

Nagasaki 15
Narcissus 39
negative energies 57-58, 68, 92
neurotic behavior 47
newspaper 63, 64
Nohavec, Janet 97
Nostradamus 4, 7, 13-15, 75, 105
Nostradame, Michel de 4, 7, 13, 75, 105

O

obsidian 11, 16
occult 18
Old, Dr. Walter Gorn 119
out of body experience 2, 36-37, 84

P

paint brush 62, 65-66
Palermo Sicily 18
paper towels 63, 68, 69
Paris 18
past lives 2, 34-35
Patras 11
Paul, St. 122
Pausanius 11
peace symbol 26
Persia 12
personal development 98
pharmacist 18
phase of the moon 100, 147, 154
Phrenology 149, 159, 170
physician 18
picture frames 62-68
Pious Fraud 47
Plague 14
Plato 160
polished stones 7
Polynesian Islands 12
portal 41
Potter, Harry 21-22, 39
prayer 80, 83-84
predictions 37, 100
Priestesses at Delphi 105
Princess Diana 15
prophecies 14

protection 57
psychic abilities 1, 5, 102-104
psychic development 28, 41, 98
psychoanalysis 47-48
psychomanteum 74-76
Pythagoras 160, 161

Q

quartz crystal 71-73, 120, 121, 146-147
quatrains 14
Queen Elizabeth I 15

R

rational mind 103-104
red wine 70
reincarnation 2, 34-35
relaxed expectation 25, 94
remote viewing 25, 36
residual energy 68-69, 92
Reunions 74
ritual 56, 57, 79-87
ritual cleansing 81
ritual clothing 81
Roman Catholic Church 14, 18, 169
Rome 19
Rowling, JK 21-22, 39

S

sage 68
St. Christopher medal 30
Saint-Remy-de-Provence 14
salt 57, 82
schizophrenia 28
Scotland 13
scrying 1, 6, 9, 70
scrying bowl 13, 70
scrying journal 100
scrying mirror 89
scrying stone 13
self-hypnosis 3, 4, 21, 38, 71, 75, 94, 95
sensory impressions 53
sensory input 21
Sepharial 119
setting your intention 29-38, 96
sexual energy 87
Shaman 12
Sibyls 161
Sicily 18
silence 90-91
skepticism 5, 45, 59, 84
skull 20
slide show 2
Smith, Joseph Jr. 20
smoke bath 68-69
smoky crystal 72
smudge 68-69
somnambulism 164
soothsayers 47
Spain 15-16
Spanish Armada 15
speculum 6, 57, 61, 95
spirit body 113-114
spirit guides 1, 26, 30-33, 39, 45, 46, 114
spirit mentors 30-33, 45, 114
Spiritualism 32, 45, 55, 58, 74, 166
Spiritualist 32, 45, 55, 58, 81, 159, 166
spirit world 9, 26, 29-30, 45, 46, 55, 56, 61, 77, 95, 114, 159
Stargate Project, the 36

subconscious mind 2, 3, 35, 47-51
sunlight 156
super-conscious mind 52-53
supernatural 10
Swedenborge, Emmanuel 121
sweet grass 68
sword blade 7
symbolism 26-27, 100, 129, 134-138

T

Talbott, Edward 16-18
Tarot cards 54
Temple of Ceres 11
Temple of Jupiter 161
Thailand 108
Theosophical movement 119
Thummin 46
Tibetan monks 83
time travel 25, 36-37, 54-55
training the mind 108-117
trance state 4, 71, 75, 94, 95, 97, 171
trickster spirits 58
Trithemius 123
Twilight Zone 43

U

unconscious mind 3, 47-53, 93, 95, 99
unintentional mirror gazing 21
universal consciousness 45, 145
universal energy source 45, 83-84
Urim 46

V

vibrations 55
visions 7, 9, 71, 132, 134
visualization 106-107, 110-117

W

waning moon 94
Washington, George 31
water 7, 14, 70, 83, 92
waxing moon 94
White House, the 21
White, John 106-107
Wiccans 80, 82
witch 46, 72, 80

X-Y-Z

www.learnancientwisdom.com

Other Books of Ancient Wisdom

The Sweat Lodge is For Everyone

ISBN 978-0-9737470-6-5 $19.95

The Native American Sweat Lodge Ceremony offers so many benefits, both spiritual and physical for anyone who has the opportunity to take part in one.

This book is the non-Native's guide to understanding, participating in, and benefiting from Native American Sweat Lodge ceremonies.

Messages in Your Tea Cup

ISBN 978-0-9783939-6-0 $19.95

Have you ever wished that you could predict the future? Throughout history people all over the world have been able to predict future events and get advice from "beyond" through tea leaf reading.

This book will teach you everything that you need to know to begin reading tea leaves immediately.

Other Books of Ancient Wisdom

Séances in Washington

ISBN 978-0-9783939-7-7 $19.95

Abraham Lincoln and Spiritualism during the Civil War.

This book is the first-hand account of the experiences of a Spiritualist medium in Washington during the Civil War. It created tremendous controversy when it was originally published in 1891, but there were enough credible witnesses to confirm her account of events that it could not be disputed.

The Spirituality of Money

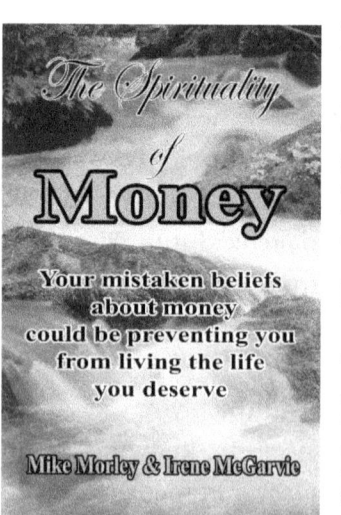

ISBN 978-0-9783939-3-9 $9.95

Does it feel like money is a constant struggle for you? We keep hearing about how easy it is to "manifest" anything we want, including money, but for most people it just isn't that easy.

This book will help you recognize the false beliefs about money that are preventing you from living the life of affluence and abundance that you deserve.

www.ingramcontent.com/pod-product-compliance
Lightning Source LLC
Chambersburg PA
CBHW061308110426
42742CB00012BA/2096